CULTURAL HERITAGE OF BENGAL

CULTURAL HERITAGE OF BENGAL:

A BIOGRAPHICAL AND CRITICAL HISTORY FROM THE EARLIEST TIMES CLOSING WITH A REVIEW OF INTELLECTUAL PROGRESS UNDER BRITISH RULE IN INDIA

R. C. DUTT

GYAN

Published by

Gyan Publishing House
5, Ansari Road
Daryaganj, New Delhi-110002
Phone: 011-47034999, 9811692060
E-mail: books@gyanbooks.com

Distribution Network
gyanbooks.com
India, USA, Canada, UK, Australia

ISBN: 978-93-6780-394-3 (PB)

First Published, 1877

2nd Impression 2025

Printed at: Gyan Press, Delhi.

CULTURAL HERITAGE OF BENGAL
Author: R. C. DUTT

CULTURAL HERITAGE OF BENGAL

CULTURAL HERITAGE OF BENGAL

A BIOGRAPHICAL AND CRITICAL HISTORY FROM THE EARLIEST TIMES CLOSING WITH A REVIEW OF INTELLECTUAL PROGRESS UNDER BRITISH RULE IN INDIA

By
R. C. DUTT

PREFACE TO THE REVISED EDITION

About twenty years ago, I published in a Calcutta magazine a series of biographical and critical essays on Bengali writers, and they were published in a collected form under the disguise of a *nom de plume* in 1877. The publication did not receive much attention at the time, but it attracted the notice of that prince of Indian statisticians, W. W. Hunter. He embodied much of the information conveyed in my book in his valuable work on the *Indian Empire,* and he suggested that a more complete treatment of the subject should be attempted.[1]

The work of bringing out a more complete work on the subject has been deferred from year to year amidst other works which have claimed my more immediate attention. I do not regret this delay, as the information available on this subject is now far more satisfactory than it was twenty years ago. More attention is now given to the study of Bengali literature by the people of Bengal; a *Bangiya Sahitya Parishad* or Academy of Bengali Literature has been formed, and it has turned its attention to the restoration of the texts of our old authors; and some excellent biographical works like the lives of Akshay Kumar Datta, Isvar Chandra Vidyasagar and Madhu Sudan Datta have lately been published in Bengali. These encouraging circumstances have reminded me of my duty,—long deferred,—of bringing out a fairly complete account of Bengali literature. And the honour which the *Bangiya Sahitya Parishad* has done me, by electing me its first President, impels me to choose this occasion to place before my countrymen generally, and before European students of Indian vernaculars, a connected story of literary and intellectual progress in Bengal during the last eight centuries.

[1] "A complete treatment of the subject is still a desideratum, which it is hoped that Bengali research will before long supply. Mr.........whose volume has been freely used in the following pages would confer a benefit both on his countrymen and on European students of the Indian vernaculars by undertaking the task."—W. W. Hunter's *Indian Empire* (1886) p. 347, *note*.

It is necessary to say one or two words about my predecessors in this field. Isvar Chandra Gupta, the first great poet of this century, an account of whose life and work will be found in Chapter XIV. of the present book, was the first writer who attempted to publish biographical accounts of previous writers; but his attempt necessarily met with imperfect success. Isvar Chandra was followed by other Bengali writers of lesser note, whose treatises used to be read in the last generation. Pandit Ramgati Nyayaratna then took up the task, and made enquiries into facts connected with the lives and writings of past authors, and produced a meritorious work a quarter of a century ago. The work has appeared in a second edition, but Bengal laments the recent death of the industrious and venerable Pandit. A number of separate biographical works, some of them very full and complete, have also been lately issued; and I have in the present edition of this work derived much information from these separate works.

The additional information now available on the subject of Bengali literature, while it is most welcome to the compiler, has made the work of compilation more arduous. I had no idea, when I undertook to produce the present edition, that nearly all the work done twenty years ago would have to be redone. But as the work proceeded, this became more and more manifest. I have accordingly virtually rewritten most portions of the book, including the first five chapters as well as the last eight chapters, and I have added two new chapters on the schools of logic and law at Nabadwip. The work therefore may be regarded as almost a new one. The very limited time I had at my disposal did not permit me to perform this work as leisurely and carefully as I would wish to do it ; but I hope nevertheless that the book will be found to be a readable hand-book, correct up to date, on the subject which it treats.

And the subject is one which is worth the study. Literary movement in Bengal commenced at least eight centuries ago with composition in Sanscrit, and Jayadeva, a native of Bengal, has left his mark on Sanscrit literature by his immortal song, now rendered into English by Sir Edwin Arnold. Bengali literature, properly so called, began with imitations of the song of Jayadeva in the fourteenth century, and with translations of the great Sanscrit epics into Bengali in the fifteenth century. Then followed the brilliant sixteenth century with its religious reform inaugurated by Chaitanya, and its study of philosophy and sacred law fostered by Raghunath and Raghunandan. The seventeenth century commenced with a great original composition by Mukunda Ram, whom E. B. Cowell of Cambridge delights to call the Chaucer of Bengal. And the eighteenth century produced Bharat Chandra a master of verse, and Ram Prasad a master of song. A brighter epoch opened with the ninteenth century; Raja Ram Mohan Roy was the first brilliant product of English education in India, and devoted his life to religious reform and to the formation of a healthy Bengali Prose. Isvar Chandra Gupta was a versatile poet and satirist, and Akshay Kumar and Vidyasagar continued the noble work which Raja Ram Mohan had commenced. The great Madhu Sudan Datta wrote a noble epic in blank verse, Dina Bandhu Mitra and others wrote dramatic works, and Bankim Chandra Chatterjee has created a new school of fiction, and has brought Bengali prose to the state of its present perfection and grace.

These are the greatest authors that Bengal has produced, and whose memory the people of Bengal love to cherish. Of living writers I have not given any detailed account; the time for a proper criticism of their work has not yet come. Let us hope that they will be the pioneers in literature in the next century, and that Bengal will shew as brilliant a record of progress in the next century as in this, which is about to close.

CUTTACK, R. C. DUTT
October, 1895.

PUBLISHER'S NOTE

This book, which in its previous edition was published under the title of *The Literature of Bengal,* from the pen of R. C. Dutt, gives, in a succinct form, an account of the origin and development of the Bengali literature down to the nineteenth century. The author also deals briefly with the outstanding contributions of Bengal to the Sanskrit poetical literature. He gives us an idea also of the Bengal Schools of Neo-Logic and Neo-Smṛti of which the greatest exponents were Raghunātha and Raghunandana respectively of mediaeval Bengal.

Dutt's is still one of the very few books from which a non-Bengali can get, within a brief compass, an idea of the intellectual life of Bengal from the remote antiquity down to the nineteenth century when the impact of western culture and civilisation brought about a renaissance in Bengal The author, an accomplished scholar, has presented the subject-matter in an elegant language and a charming style.

The Literature of Bengal, which is so useful a work written by such an able and distingushed scholar, has long been out of print. For the benefit of the general readers we are publishing a reprint of the revised edition of the book. In the reprint we have kept the text intact. For considerations of space some of the excerpts, quoted in the footnotes, have been reduced ; in doing so care has been taken not to omit any relevant portion. For facility in printing and convenience of the readers, who are not familiar with the Bengali script, the Bengali quotations, have been transliterated into the Roman script. It should be added that the book, having been composed in the ninteenth century, contained much information that is at variance with the results of up-to-date researches. In such cases, up-to-date information has been given in the footnotes as editor's remarks.

It is expected that this reprint will satisfy the needs of those for whom it is intended.

BIOGRAPHICAL NOTE

Ramesh Chunder Dutt, President, Fifteenth Indian National Congress, 1899, the historian, poet, novelist, politician, statesman, litterateur and linguist was born in 1948 in Calcutta, and belonged to the well-known Rambagan Dutt family of which several members distinguished themselves as poets and writers, notably his uncle Soshi Chunder Dutt, a prolific writer whose works ran into ten volumes and whose mastery of the English language and grace of style attracted the notice of competent critics; and but for the cruel hand of fate we might have had in his niece Taru Dutt, whose command over both the English and French languages was all but miraculous, a poetess whose verses would have ranked her among the immortals of Parnassus.

When Govin Dutt, father of Taru Dutt, published in 1870 *The Dutt Family Album* from England, it sprung a surprise upon the English reading public. It is a remarkable book of 197 English verses of which 139 pieces were contributed by the members of the Dutt family.

In 1864 when reading for his degree examination Ramesh Chunder Dutt ran away from home with B. L. Gupta and Surendra Nath Banerjea to England and passed the open competion for the Indian Civil Service in 1869. For twenty years, from 1871 to 1897, he served as a distinguished member of the Indian Civil Service in various parts of Bengal, Bihar and Orissa.

He had not been three years in service when he tried his hand at fiction-writing and during 1874-85 he brought out a series of six Bengali social and historical novels. Not content, however, with writing works of fiction, he betook himself to the hard soil of history and produced a number of historical works. In 1885 he translated and published in Bengali the *Rig-veda* and a few years later a selection from the ancient sacred literature of the Hindus in two ponderous volumes which he named the *Hindu Shastras.*

Besides being a consummate scholar of Sanskrit and knowing French, German, Persian, Hindi, Urdu and Oriya, Dutt's industry was remarkable, for in addition to his numerous books he was a frequent contributor to principal reviews and literary magazines. He was also a journalist of no mean reput having acted from 1899-1901 as a Special Correspondent of the *Indian Mirror*, a daily newspaper of Calcutta.

It may be that when English is a dead language, Dutt's writings may be reckoned by scholars to count with a work of an Apuleius or a Fronto. It is an astonishingly interesting example of the clothing of Hindu ideas with English phrases. Nothing is more difficult than to translate religious phraseology. Sanscrit, we are told, owes much of its copious vocabulary to the variety of religious and ethical ideas which it strove to put into words. Bengali, of all the modern vernaculars of India, is the most Sanscritised—a charateristic which has drawn upon it the criticism of linguists accustomed to tongues in which the Sanscrit element has been softened and modified. It is not for a foreigner to contest the justness of such criticisms. But one result has evidently followed—the Bengali language is charged with Hindu sentiment, and Bengali literature is essentially a Hindu literature. Hindi has evolved, in Urdu, a Mahomedan dialect rich in Persian and Arabic words, and turns of phrase suitable for the expression of Muslim ideas. But Bengali, in spite of the fact that in some of the Eastern districts of the province three-fourths of the population is Mahomedan, remains a Hindu speech, and can hardly give expression to religious sentiments and ideas save in words round which cling the associations of the Puranas. Hence a Bengali, no matter how extensive his Western reading, thinks in an essentially Hinduised speech, and is, as we say, a Hindu "at heart." So was it certainly with Dutt. He attempted what was, perhaps, an impossible task. The very metres of Bengali, its extraordinary richness of rhyme and fluency of rhythm, made it terribly difficult to reproduce a similar effect of sound and sentiment in our more stubborn and less lyrical tongue. We can hardly wonder that in later life, Mr. Dutt turned to the easier task of rendering Sanskrit verse into English —assiduous practice had given him a completer control over his second language (for Sanskrit must practically have formed part of his native speech), and Dutt's versions of the Vedic hymns are graceful and easy. We can only respectfully admire a linguistic talent which is rare indeed in our own race. But we must not be led into the belief that this linguistic versatility, this instinctive comprehension and grasp of foreign phrase and idiom, reflected a loose cosmopolitanism of thought. As in the case of that other Dutt, the famous Madhu Sudhan, an European education only sharpened and heightened the innate appreciation of Hindu imagination, the copious inventiveness of Hindu fancy in the poetical treatment of religious thought. For a time it was natural that Dutt should come under the influence of his official surroundings and his European colleagues. But advancing years take us back irresistably to hereditary influences, and it was inevitable that, in the autumn of his days, one who was essentially Hindu in thought and aspiration should more and more reflect the current ideas of his race. His renewed belief in the Permanent Settlement was, after all, very natural in one whose family were Zemindars under Lord Cornwallis's famous Regulations.

Perhaps we may be permitted to regret that Dutt made only one early incursion into composition in his native tongue. In English he doubtless addressed a wider and more influential audience. His ready eloquence in spoken English was marvellous—so apt and unerring was his choice of phrase. It would be interesting to learn under what impulses he turned, not without some reluctance we may be sure, to the popularisation in the West of the treasures of Hindu thought, and the rendering into English words of the subtle allusiveness of Hindu poetry. Few Indians can have been more Eurapeanised in sympathy and intelligence, none can have remained more constant to the Hindu ideals, and to the Hindu fertility of imagination, which is the birthright of his race.

His mother-land owes him a debt of gratitude for the manner in which he has enriched her literature. As an Official and as an Historian he had very strong views on the system of permanent settlement, and on the condition of the peasantry. Some of these views he modified in later life. He thus laid himself open to the charge of inconsistency. But consistency is, at best, a doubtful virtue, and honest change of view has characterised some of our most distinguished men. Second thoughts are often best, and third thoughts frequently prove a riper first.

"Fierce light" beat upon Romesh Chandra's career from the very first, but, though he must often have felt nervous, his character stood the test, and as Prime Minister to the Gaekwar he finally proved his fitness for "highest trust."

It is not merely as a literary man and a politician that Dutt figures high among his countrymen, but also as a quiet, unobtrusive social reformer. He has a right to be given a high place in the ranks of social reformer for the silent work he has done without indulging in the claptrap platform verbosity of many modern so-called reform leaders. He is one of those men who believed in reforms, like charity, beginning at home.

Among his works are: *Three Years in Europe* (1872), *The Peasantry of Bengal* (1875), *The Literature of Bengal* (1877), *Lays of Ancient India* (1893), *History of Civilization of Ancient India: 3 vols.* (*1890*), *England and India* (1897), *The Mahabharata* (English versical translation, with Introduction by Maxmuller), (1898), *The Ramayana* (In English verse) (1899), *Famines in India* (1900) and *Economic History of British India,* 2 vols. (1902).

He died while acting as Prime Minister of Baroda in 1909.

CONTENTS

CHAPTER I

Bengali Language and Alphabet

It is not difficult to trace the gradual changes in the spoken tongue of Northern India by the help of the ancient works which have been preserved in Sanscrit. In India, as elsewhere, political and religious changes have been attended, not with sudden changes in the spoken tongue, as is sometimes imagined, but with a sudden recognition of such changes which introduce themselves slowly enough.

When the vigorous colonists of the Epic Age left their mother country in the Punjab behind, and founded powerful kingdoms along the Ganges and the Jumna, the Sanscrit of the *Rig Veda* was replaced by the Sanscrit of the *Brahmanas* and *Upanishads* in the cultured courts of the Kurus and the Panchalas, the Videhas and the Kosalas. This was the first change of which we have any recorded evidence, and we may roughly fix the date of this change at 1500 B. C.

With the rise of Magadha and the advent of Gautama Buddha, who preferred to preach to nations in the spoken tongue,[1] the Pali language was recognized as the spoken tongue of Northern India ;[2] it had replaced the Sanscrit of the *Brahmanas* and *Upanishads*. Scholars generally agree with Burnouf and Lassen that the Pali stands "on the first step of the ladder of departure from Sanscrit, and is the first of the series of dialects which break us that rich and fertile language." The date of the literary and general recognition of the Pali language may be roughly fixed at 500 B. C.

In the centuries following the Christian Era, the Pali became gradually replaced by the Prakrits, the spoken dialects of the people. The heroines of Kalidasa speak Prakrit; and while Dushyanta makes love in Sanscrit, the beauteous Sakuntala responds to his love in the softer Prakrit. Vararuchi, one

[1] cf. *anujānāmi bhikkhave sakāya*
niruttiyā buddha-vacanam pariyāpunitum. — Ed.

[2] For the origin and homeland of Pāli, see B. C. Law : *A History of Pāli Literature*, Vol. I, Introduction.—Ed.

of the "nine gems" of Vikramaditya's court, is the earlist grammarian who recognizes the Prakrits in his grammar ;[3] and he distinguishes four distinct dialects of the Prakrit, *viz.*, *Maharashtri*, *Sauraseni*, *Paisachi* and *Magadhi*. We may fix the date of this literary recognition of the Prakrit dialects at 500 A. D.

The different Prakrits have been modified[4] into the different spoken dialects of modern India. It is probable that the *Maharashtri* and *Sauraseni* Prakrits have been modified into the modern Hindi, and that the *Magadhi* Prakrit has been modified into the modern Bengali. Hindi received literary recognition in the twelfth century after Christ, the Bengali in the fourteenth century.[5]

If we take up any large number of colloquial Bengali words derived from the Sanscrit, we shall invariably find in them traces of the Prakrit. If we take up any sentence at random from our every-day conversation, we shall find that most of the words have been derived from the Sanscrit, through the Prakrit. We subjoin in a foot-note a list of words, furnished by Pandit Ramgati Nyayaratna, which will shew at a glance that the Bengali language is immediately derived from the Prakrit.[6]

[3] *Prākṛta-prakāśa.*—Ed.

[4] Through Apabhraṁśa.—Ed.

[5] Later researches have unearthed the Bengali work *Bauddha Gān O Dohā* (also called *Caryāpada*) which is generally assigned to a period between the 10th and the 12th century A.D.—Ed.

[6] The process of evolution of some Bengali words from Sanskrit through Prākṛta is given below :

Sanskrit	Prākṛta	Bengali
asti	*acchi*	*āche*
adya	*ajja*	*āj*
kathayati	*kahai*	*kahe*
kārya	*kajja*	*kāj*
gṛha	*ghara*	*ghara*
candra	*canda*	*cānd*
nṛtyati	*naccai*	*nāce*
patati	*paḍai*	*paḍe*
bhakta	*bhatta*	*bhāta*
vatsa	*vaccha*	*vāchā*
śmaśāna	*masāna*	*maśāna*
sandhyā	*sañjhā*	*sāñjh*
hasta	*hattha*	*hāta*

The Bengali language is thus a descendant of Sanscrit, the mother of languages. It should be remembered however that a large number of local words, which were probably used in Bengal before the Aryans asserted their possession and spread their language in this country, have found their way into the Bengali tongue. Many familiar Bengali words connected with fishing and cultivation, with manufacture and arts, with domestic life and occupations, cannot be traced to Sanscrit roots, and must be of indigenous origin.[7] With the growth of literature however these words have a tendency to disappear, and the Bengali language is gradually approximating to the Sanscrit in various ways.

This process is specially observable in the present century. Whoever has taken pains to compare the best works of the present age with the works of the last century, must have observed that the Sanscrit element has greatly increased in the Bengali of the present day; and this change,—and we consider it a change in the right direction,—is attributable to a variety of causes. The spread of Europtan culture created the necessity of a prose literature. Our writers began to be familiarized with ideas which could not find expression in verse. Philosophy and the sciences came within the category of public tuition, and were learnt by an ever-increasing circle of students; and when they wanted to give expression to their ideas in their mother tongue they found out its inadequacy. Philosophy and the sciences were in past centuries cultivated in the academies of Nadia, but they were cultivated in Sanscrit, only by a few, and those few never conceived the idea of popularizing and spreading such knowledge. A more liberal spirit however was imbibed in this century from the West, and those who imbibed such notions were led to spread and popularize the knowledge they had obtained. One of the first and foremost too who received such notions was the great Raja Ram Mohan Roy, whose life was devoted to religious reform as well as to the spread of knowledge; and Ram Mohan Roy is *the father of Prose Literature in Bengal.*

[7] Such words are called *Deśī*, e.g., *ḍāb*, *ḍiṅgi*, *ḍhol* etc. The other kinds of words, constituting the Bengali vocabulary, are *Tat-sama* (similar to Sanskrit) and *Tad-bhava* (derived from Sanskrit).—Ed.

It was then that two great authors, Akshay Kumar Datta and Isvar Chandra Vidyasagar, took up the subject; and it may we asserted truly that as Ram Mohan Roy formed the prose literature of Bengal, Akshay Kumar and Isvar Chandra gave it its classical dress. They had few or no instruments to work with, they had no style before them on which to base their own, none to follow or imitate. Under such circumstances they turned their eyes to the Sanskrit language. That wonderful language is the richest in the world in its capacity for the formation of new terms from known roots; and the twin workers borrowed vastly from this store and developed Bengali prose.

Since that time the same causes have continued to operate. New ideas are daily imported from the West, and are entering into the spirit of our literature. We seek in vain for expressions suited to such ideas in our older works, and we naturally turn more and more to the Sanscrit, and borrow from that language. Michael Madhu Sudan, the greatest poet of the century, borrowed largely from Sanscrit. And Bankim Chandra, the greatest master of the Bengali prose, simplified the classical style of Akshay Kumar and Vidyasagar and made it more pliable and graceful, but his indebtedness to Sanscrit was not less than that of his predecessors. A comparison of a poem of the present century with one of the past century will at once indicate the difference.

We open a book before us at random, and find a poem entitled *Usha* in the *Sraban* number of the *Banga-Darsan,* 1280 B. E.[8] It begins thus:

> *aditi-nandīnī, ūṣā vinodinī,*
> *praphulla-vadanā, madhura-bhāṣiṇī,*
> *āloka-vasanā, kusuma-mālinī,*
> *esa tumi devi, avanī-tale* ||

With the exception of two words only, *esa* and *tumi* all the rest are Sanscrit words.

We turn over a few pages and come to another poem entitled *deva-nidra* in the *Bhadra number.* It begins thus:—

[8] This portion was written in July 1874, and the quotations therefore are from the *Banga-Darśan* of 1280 B. E.

kona mahāmati mānava-santān,
bujhite vidhir śāsan vidhān,
adhīr haila vāsanānale,
* * * *
dekhiva bhāsiche kārṇa-jale||

In these lines there are only four words which are not Sanskrit, *kona, bujhite, haila* and *dekhiva.* All the other words are Sanscrit, though some of them have Bengali terminations. The four words above mentioned are of course derived from Sanskrit roots.

The *Asvin* number has no poetry, and we therefore turn to the *Kartik* number. The poem on *Vāyu* begins thus:

janma mama sūrya-teje,
* * * *
yathā ḍāke megha-rāśi,
* * * *
vijali jvale|

In these lines only two words *ḍāke* and *vijali* are not Sanscrit. The terminations are Bengali of course.

In the lines which we have quoted above, there are only eight words which are not Sanscrit. We now turn to the poetry of the last century, and select a passage at random from Bharat Chandra's *Annada Mangal*:

kahe sakhī jayā śuna go abhayā
e ki kare ṭhākurāli ||
krodhe kari bhar yāve vāp-ghar
kheyāti have kāṅgāli||
* * * *
jananīr āśe yāve piṭṛ-vāse
bhāje dive sadā tāḍā||
vāpe nā jijñāse māye nā sambhāṣe
yadi dekhe lakṣmī-chāḍā||

Our readers will see at a glance that most of the words in this passage are non-Sanscrit, although mostly derived from Sanscrit roots.

We have dwelt at some length on this change because it is a change of which we should take note. The Bengali language, though undoubtedly derived through the Prakrit, seems to be fast divesting itself of the Prakrit forms, and approximating to the Sanscrit. The modern tendency is to use Sanscrit words rather than their Prakrit forms in all works of literature, except dramas and light fiction. To select some words from Pandit Nyayaratna's list, we prefer *prastar* to *pāthar*, *cakra* to *cākā*, *adya* to *āj*, *hasta* to *hāt*, *snāna* to *nāhā* in our literary works. The literary language is thus undergoing a transformation under our own eyes.

It would be a mistake however to suppose that we are imitating Sanscrit ideas. The reverse is rather the case, our notions, our ideas, our ways of thinking, our style of writing are day by day diverging from the classical Sanscrit model, and tending towards the European. It is words only that we are borrowing from the Sanscrit. Thus, at the same time, we are borrowing from two widely different sources.

We have now briefly indicated the origin of the Bengali language and its development in modern times. It remains now to make a few remarks with regard to the Bengali alphabet.

A cursory examination of the Bengali alphabet will convince our readers that it is derived and simplified from the Devanagari alphabet. This modification was made many centuries ago, and all that exists of Bengali literature from the time of Chandi Das and Kasiram Das was recorded in this modern Bengali alphabet.

But this does not take us to the origin of the Indian alphabet. The Devanagari character itself is of comparatively recent origin. The oldest Indian character known is not the Devangari, but the older one in which Asoka's inscriptions are recorded. All the inscriptions of Asoka, except those in the Punjab, are recorded in what is called the *Indo-Pali* or *South Asoka* character. This is the earliest character used in India of which we have any knowledge now, and its date is the date of Asoka, *viz.*, the third century before Christ.

The late General Sir Alexander Cunningham, who was the greatest authority on the subject of the Indian alphabets, subjected the old *Indo-Pali* character to a careful examination, and came to the conclusion that this Indian character was of purely Indian origin.[9] And the majority of scholars who have studied and discussed the subject are of the same opinion. Professor Max Müller holds that India had no written alphabet befort the fifth century B.C., and that the Indian alphabet was then borrowed from the West. But Dr. Roth expresses his conviction, based on prolonged Vedic studies, that the vast collection of Vedic hymns could not possibly have depended for existence on oral transmission, and he considers it as a *sine quâ non* that writing was known in Vedic times. Dr. Bühler holds that the Indian alphabet with its five nasals and three sibilants must have been developed in the grammatical schools of the Brahmans. Dr. Goldstücker holds that writing was known when the Vedic hymns were composed. And the profound scholar Lassen maintains that the *Indo-Pali* alphabet is of purely indigenous Indian origin.

It would appear therefore that some alphabet was formed and developed in India in the Vedic times; that probably a later modification of this alphabet is the *Indo-Pali* character in which Asoka recorded his inscriptions in the third century B. C.; that the ornate *Devanagari* character was a later development of the simpler and older *Indo-Pali* character; and that the *Bengali* character is a simplification and later modification of the Devanagari character.

[9] See Cunningham's remarks on this subject quoted in my *Civilization in Ancient India* (London, 1893) Vol. II., p. 25 *et seq.*

CHAPTER II

EARLY SANSCRIT POETRY: JAYADEVA

A GREAT development in Sanscrit literature and learning took place between the sixth and eighth centuries of the Christian Era, and all the writers who are known as Classical Sanscrit poets, and whose works are still popular in all parts of India, appear to have flourished in this age. Kalidasa took the lead, probably in the sixth century,[1] in poetry and in drama, and was immediately succeeded by Bharavi. Harshadeva, Dandin, Banabhatta, Subandhu and Bhartrihari wrote dramas, fiction and poetry in the seventh, and the immortal Bhavabhuti closed the bright list in the eighth.[2] Classical poetry ends with him, imitators and feeble writers rose later on. Such were Magha who wrote *Sisupalabadha* in the eleventh century,[3] and Visakha Datta who composed *Mudra Rakshasa* when the Musalmans were already in India.[4]

Bengal does not come to notice by her literary work till this late period. It is said that Bhatta Narayana who composed *Veni Sanhara* was one of the Brahmans who came to Bengal from Kanouj in the time of king Adisura, but we know little of the king and less of the poet. And it is also said that Sri Harsha who composed *Naishadha* in the twelfth century lived in Bengal, although according to Rajasekhara he was born in Benares.

The earliest poet whom we can claim to be a true son of Bengal was Jayadeva, the composer of the immortal song *Gita*

[1] Kālidāsa is generally supposed by modern scholars to have flourished round about 400 A.D. Aśvaghoṣa, a pre-Kālidāsa poet, is usually assigned to Kaniṣka's time (c. 1st century B.C. or A.D.).—Ed.

[2] For an account of Classical Sanscrit Poetry, Drama and Fiction see my *Civilization in Ancient India*, (London, 1893) Vol. II. pp. 258 to 302. Also see A. B. Keith : *History of Sanskrit Literature*, Oxford, 1928, and S. K. De : *History of Sanskrit Literature*, Calcutta, 1947. —Ed.

[3] According to later researches, Māgha must have been earlier than 8th—9th century A.D.—Ed.

[4] He is now generally supposed to have flourished earlier than the 9th century A.D.—Ed.

Govinda; and we will devote the present chapter to an account of the life and works of this earliest poet of Bengal.[5] He was a poet of the court of Lakshmana Sena, and flourished in the twelfth century, as has been proved by a colophon of an ancient copy of his poem discovered by Dr. Bühler in Kashmir. There is other evidence corroborating this fact. Jayadeva himself speaks of his contemporaries in his poetry; Bidyapati and Chandidas, poets of the fourteenth century, acknowledge Jayadeva to be their great predecessor; and Sanatana, a learned Vaishnava writer of the sixteenth century, speaks of Jayadeva as a poet of Lakshmana Sena's time.

Very little is known of the life of this, the earliest poet of Bengal. He was born in Kendubilva, better known as Kenduli, in the district of Birbhum. His father's name was Bhojadeva, and his mother's Bamadevi. In early life Jayadeva left home, and it is said, began preaching the faith and love of Krishna. He had a few pupils and followers, and it is asserted that he attempted to establish a reformed religion like what Chaitanya did four centuries later. All this, however, we must accept with caution. Much of what little we know of Jayadeva is from Vaishnava writers, and they were naturally anxious to discover and establish a resemblance between so great a poet and their great Master. That Jayadeva's faith in Krishna was ardent and deep, is amply shewn in his great work; that the same fervour was shared, not only by a few friends of his, but by a large portion of the people at large, is also highly probable; but that he began preaching the faith of Krishna like Chaitanya is perhaps the unfounded supposition of later Vaishnava writers.

After passing a few years in devotion and study, Jayadeva married and settled down in his native village. The daily routine of home life was however ill adapted to the feelings of the ardent poet, and he left home once more and travel-

[5] A poet named Abhinanda, with the word 'Gauḍa' prefixed to his name, is supposed by some to have flourished in Bengal about the 9th century A.D. Sandhyākara Nandin, the author of the 'Rāma-carita' was a Bengali who probably lived between the last quarter of the 11th century and the middle of the 12th. So, Jayadeva who flourished towards the end of the 12th century cannot be said to have been the earliest poet of Bengal.—Ed.

led through northern India as far as Vrindavan and Jaypur, to which latter place he seems to have been invited by the king. Nothing more is known of the poet than that he survived his wife Padmavati, and that he passed his last days in devotions in his native village, where his tomb is yet to be seen surrounded by beautiful groves and trees.

The little that is known of the life of the poet is so mixed up with fables, that it is impossible at this distance of time to glean the truth from the falsehood. Such fables, however, are often based on true facts or circumstances; anyhow they represent the impressions of later ages regarding the life and times of their subject. As such, some of them may with propriety find a place in this brief sketch.

A curious story is connected with the marriage of Jayadeva with Padmavati. A certain childless Brahman, after many prayers and devotions, was favoured by the god Jagannatha with an only girl, whom the father named Padmavati and nursed with affection and care. When she attained her youth, her father was taking her to the god, intending to devote her to his services. In the way however he dreamt a dream, and the god told him to give his child in marriage to a certain devout follower of his, named Jayadeva. The Brahman did as this match-making god commanded. Jayadeva, then leading a life of study and devotions, was unwilling to encumber himself with a wife; but the girl would not leave him, and said she would follow him through life though forsaken. "One must love partridge very well to accept it when thrown in one's face," the sort of feeling one would naturally feel under such circumstances, but our poet knew better; he rewarded her persistent affections with marriage, and they made a very affectionate and happy couple ever after in life.

The death of Padmavati furnishes us with another story. She is said to have been so affectionate a wife that a false rumour of her husband's death caused her death. Such virtue however dwelt in the name of Krishna, that the poet had no sooner muttered that name than his spouse woke to life again.

The most celebrated story however, connected with the poet's life, is that relating to the composition of a certain passage in the 10th *Sarga* of the *Gita Govinda*. The passage occurs where Krishna is represented as pacifying the wrath of Radhika, who had been offended with him for his promiscuous love, and had assumed a contemptuous silence towards him. *mama śirasi maṇḍanam dehi pada-pallavamudāram* means, "On my head, as an ornament, place your beauteous feet,"— these words being a touching appeal which an offended mistress seldom resists. When Jayadeva composed this, he looked on Krishna as an ardent lover; but after he had written the first portion, *viz.,* "On my head, as an ornament," he remembered that Krishna was a god as well; and he hesitated to add any thing about a human foot being placed on the head of a deity. Filled with doubts the poet went to bathe in the river. Soon after Padmavati saw her husband return and ask for his meals. The breakfast was produced and finished, and then he went to the room where the *Gita Govinda* was kept, and wrote something. After her husband had finished his meals, the duteous wife finished hers, when lo! her husband came in again and called for breakfast. The worthy dame certainly did not relish this unseasonable joke, but her husband was obstinate, and asserted that he had only then returned from his bath and had not yet taken his meals. The confusion of poor Padmavati would have been complete, but she stated that he had just before added something to his book. The book was examined, and what was the poet's surprise when he found that after the words, "On my head, as an ornament," which he had written before, the words "place thy beauteous feet" had been added. The mystery was soon cleared up. The god Krishna had marked the doubts which had arisen in the mind of his votary, and had solved the difficulty by personally assuming the shape of Jayadeva, coming into his house, and writing the passage himself.

There is more in this story than at first sight meets the eye. The real hesitation felt at the passage was not by Jayadeva, but by later Vaishnavas who regarded Krishna as God, and the story was invented to explain away the poet's audacity.

It is said, that the king of Nilachala was offended at the widely spreading fame of Jayadeva, and wrote a book on the same subject and challenged comparison. Learned Pandits, unable or unwilling to decide the question, placed both the volumes at the temple of Jagannatha, calling upon the deity to decide it. It is said that the deity held the volume of Jayadeva on his breast, and threw away the work of king Satvika. Posterity has sufficiently vindicated the critical powers of the deity. Centuries have rolled away and the fame of Jayadeva remains undiminished, and will continue to remain so long as the Sanscrit language is not forgotten.

Centuries have rolled away since the death of Jayadeva, and yet to the present day an annual fair is held at Kenduli by the Vaishnavas in memory of the departed poet. At this fair, fifty or sixty thousand men assemble round the tomb of Jayadeva for worship, and the Vaishnavas still sing of the amours of Krishna and Radhika immortalized in the *Gita Govinda*.

The Bengali was no doubt the spoken tongue of Bengal at the time of Jayadeva, as it is now. But the learned and the *elite* still considered the Sanscrit tongue as their noble heritage, and authors vied with each other in writing in this language. All learned works, therefore, all speeches in court, all traditional and genealogical fables, were composed and recited in Sanscrit. Learned Brahmans carried on their investigations in this learned language, and poets, desirous of ingratiating themselves with kings, composed and pronounced stiff artificial poetry in a dead language. It was thus that the Italians of the age of Dante and Boccacio wrote in Latin ; it was thus that Anglo-Saxon writers of the time of the great Alfred made feeble attempts in the language of Rome. All attempts in a foreign tongue or in a dead tongue must necessarily be feeble ; and thus with the single exception of Jayadeva's works, all compositions of the twelfth century have been forgotten, and deservedly forgotten.

The *Gita Govinda*, however, is an exception, and a noble exception. It is a book of songs on the amours of Krishna and Radhika, divided into twelve *Sargas* or Cantos, each *Sarga* being divided into several *Prabandhas*, and each *Prabandha* consisting of several verses. The first thing that strikes the reader in this poem is the exquisite music of the songs. One would suppose the sonorous and somewhat artificial Sanscrit language was unsuited to so much softness and melody; but it is a master hand that wakes the lyre, and the ear is pleased and ravished with a flood of the softest music before one comprehends the sense. In the hand of a *Bengali* poet the Sanscrit language loses its august stiffness and asumes more than Italian softness; and constant yet melodious repetitions and alliterations make the *Gita Govinda* a remarkable and singular work in the Sanscrit language.

And if the book is rich in its music, it is no less rich in its descriptions. The blue waves of the Jumna, the cool shade of the Tamal tree, the soft whisperings of the Malaya breeze, the voluptuous music of Krishna's flute, the timid glances of the love-stricken milk-maids, the fond workings of a lover's heart, the pangs of jeolousy, the sorrows of separation, the raptures of re-union,—all these are clearly and vividly described in the song of the immortal bard of Birbhum.

The poem begins with a description of love-lorn milk-maids disporting themselves around Krishna in the cool shades of Gokul. Radhika sees this; she marks with bitter pang the love of Krishna shared by less worthy rival's; and yet the very sight of Krishna half tempers her sorrow. Nothing can be more beautiful than the description of the joy and delight which the forlorn and abandoned Radha feels, involuntarily and almost in spite of herself, at the very sight of him who is so dear to her heart. An English version conveys no idea of the beauty and softness of the oiginal, yet such as it is, we quote from Sir William Jones's translation:—

"That god whose cheek is beautified by the nectar of his smiles, whose pipe drops in his ecstacy, I saw in the groves encircled by the damsels of Vraja who gazed on him askance from the corners of his eyes. I saw him in the grove with happier damsels, yet the sight of him delighted me. Soft is the gale which breathes over yon clear pool, and expands clustering blossoms of the voluble Asoka—soft yet grievous to me in the absence of the foe of Madhu. Delightful are the flowers of Amra trees on the mountain tops while the murmuring bees pursue their voluptuous toil,—delightful yet affecting to me O! friend, in the absence of the youthful Kesava."[6]

[6] *hasta-srasta-vilāsa-vaṁśamanṛjubhru-vallimadballavī-
vṛndotsāri-dṛganta-vīkṣitam ati-svedārdra-gaṇḍasthalam |
māmudvīkṣya vilajjitam smita-sudhā-mugdhānanam kānane
govindam vraja-sundarī-gaṇa-vṛtam paśyāmi hṛṣyāmi ca ||
durāloka-stoka-stabaka-navakāśoka-latikā-*

In the sorrow of her heart Radhika retires into her grove and weeps. There the Duti sees her and describes to her afresh the amours of Krishna. Radha's heart bleeds afresh, and the workings of a jealous mind are powerfully described by our author. We will quote one passage in which she concludes a touching and bitter lamentation:—

"O, gale, scented with sandal, who breathest love from the regions of the south, be propitious but for a moment: when thou hast brought my beloved before my eyes thou mayst freely waft away my soul! Love, with eyes like blue water-lilies, again assails me and triumphs, and while the perfidy of my beloved rends my heart, my female friend is my foe, the cool breeze scorches me like a flame, and the nectar-dropping moon is my poison. Bring disease and death, O! gale of Malaya! seize my spirit, O! god with five arrows! I ask not mercy from thee: no more will I dwell in the cottage of my father. Receive me into thy azure waves, O! sister Yamuna, that the ardour of my heart may be allayed!"[7]

But the hour of retribution comes at last. The *Duti* goes back of Krishna, and describes to him the wretched state to which he has brought his beloved. Krishna is seized with compunction, seeks out Radhika, and tries to pacify her wrath by a touching entreaty and appeal. The appeal is too lengthy for quotation, we quote a portion of it[8]:—

vikāśaḥ kāsāroparana-pavano'pi vyathayati |
api bhrāmyad bhṛṅgī-raṇita-ramaṇīyā na mukula-
prasūtiścūtānām sakhi śikhariṇīyam sukhayati ||

—*Gita Govinda*, 2nd *Sarga*. Our quotations are made from Haridas Hirachand's edition of the *Gita Govinda*. The above translation must have been from some other edition as slight differences are observable.

[7] *manobhavānandana candanānila*
prasīda re dakṣiṇa muñca vāmatām |
kṣaṇam jagat-prāṇa vidhāya mādhavam
puro mama prāṇa-haro bhaviṣyasi ||

[8] *ripuriva sakhī-samvāso'yam śikhīva himānilo*
viṣamiva sudhā-raśmi dūram dunoti manogate |
hṛdayamadaye tasminnevam punar valate balāt
kuvalayadṛśām vāmaḥ kāmo nikāmaniraṅkuśaḥ ||
rādhām vidhehi malayānila pañcavāṇa
prāṇān gṛhāṇa na gṛhan punarāśrayiṣye |
kim te kṛtāntābhagini kṣamayā taraṅgai
raṅgāṇi siñca mama śāmyatu deha-dāhaḥ ||

—Gita Govinda, 7th Sarga.

"Speak but one mild word, and the rays of thy sparkling teeth will dispel the gloom of my fears. My trembling lips like thirsty *chatakas* long to drink the moon-beams of thy cheek. O! my darling, who art naturally so tender-hearted, abandon thy causeless indignation. At this moment the flame of desire consumes my heart, O! grant me a draught of honey from the lotus of thy mouth. Or if thou beest inexhorable, grant me death from the arrows of thy keen eyes; make thy arms my chains, and punish me according to thy pleasure. Thou art my life, thou art my ornament, thou art a pearl in the ocean of my mortal birth; O! be favourable now, and my heart shall eternally be grateful. Thine eyes, which nature formed like blue water-lilies, are become through thy resentment like petals of the crimson lotus; O! tinge with their effulgence these my dark limbs that they may glow like the shafts of love tipped with flowers. Place on my head that foot like a fresh leaf, and shade me from the sun of thy passion whose beams I am unable to bear. Spread a string of gems on those two soft globes; let the golden bells of thy zone tinkle and proclaim the mild edict of love! Say, O! damsel, with delicate speech, shall I dye red with the juice of *alaktaka* those beautiful feet which will make the full-blown land-lotus blush with shame?"[9]

[9] *vadasi yadi kimcidapi danta-ruci-kaumudi*
harati dara-timiram atighoram|
sphuradadhara-sīdhave tava vadana-candramā
rocayati locana-cakoram||
priye cāru-śīle priye cāru-sīle
muñca mayi mānam anidānam|
sapadi madanānalo dahati mama mānasam
dehi mukha-kamala-madhupānam||
satyamevāsi yadi sumati mayi kopāni
dehi khara-nayana-śarāghātam|
ghaṭaya bhuja-bandhanam janaya rada-khaṇḍanam
yena vā bhavati sukha-jātam||
tvamasi mama bhūṣaṇam tvamasi mama jīvanam
tvamasi mama bhava-jaladhi-ratnam|
bhavatu bharatiha mayi satatam anurodhinī
tatra mama hṛdayam atiyatnam||
nīla-nalinābhamapi tanvi tava locanam
dhārayati kokanada-rūpam|
kusuma-śara-bāṇa-bhāvena yadi rañjayasi

Who can resist such a touching, glowing appeal, and from such a handsome appellant? Radhika could not. If she had proper cause of offence, the offender has done proper penance, and all resentment is at an end. Krishna retires to his grove, and Radhika follows him, and is thus welcomed with an outburst of passionate welcome.

"Enter, sweet Radha, the bower of Hari; seek delight, O! thou whose bosom laughs with the foretaste of happiness.

Enter, sweet Radha, the bower graced with a bed of Asoka leaves; seek delight, O! thou whose garland leaps with joy on thy breast.

Enter, sweet Radha, the bower illumined with sweet blossoms; seek delight, O! thou whose limbs far excel them in softness.

Enter, O! Radha, the bower made cool and fragrant by gales from the woods of Malaya; seek delight, O! thou whose amorous lays are softer than breezes.

Enter, O! Radha, the bower spread with leaves of twining creepers; seek delight, O! thou whose arms have been so long inflexible.

Enter, O! Radha, the bower which resounds with the murmur of honey-making bees; seek delight, O! thou whose embrace yields more equisite sweetness.

Enter, O! Radha, the bower attuned by the melodious band of Kokilas; seek delight, O! thou whose lips, which out-

kṛṣṇam-idam-etad-anurūpam||
sphuratu kuca-kumbhayor-upari maṇi-mañjari
rañjayatu tava hṛdaya-deśam|
rasatu raśanāpi tava ghana-jaghana-maṇḍale
ghoṣayatu manmatha-nideśam||
sthala-kamala-gañjanam mama hṛdaya-rañjanam
janita-rati-raṅga-parabhāgam|
bhaṇa masṛṇa-vāṇi karavāṇi caraṇa-dvayam
sarasa-lasad-alaktaka-rāgam||
smara-garala-khaṇḍanam mama śirasi maṇḍanam
dehi pada-pallavam udāram|
jvalati mayi dāruṇo madana-kadanānalo
haratu tadupahita-vikāram||

—Gita Govinda, 10th Sarga

shine the grains of the pomegranate, are embellished when thou speakest by the brightness of thy teeth.[10]

Here we must pause. The pleasures of a re-union between two such amiable and enthusiastic lovers may be better conceived than described even by the inimitable Jayadeva. Enough has been said to indicate the character and merits of Jayadeva's poetry. He is the only poet in Bengal who has attained eminence by writing in a dead language, who has wrung such soft melody out of an artificial classical language, who has embalmed and perpetuated the amours of Radha and Krishna in songs which remain as the sole specimen of lyrical composition in Sanskrit literature.

We may here mention some scholars have discovered in the *Gita Govinda* a concealed allegory. The joys of Krishna in company with the milkmaids of Brindaban represent earthly pleasures which seduce our heart and lull our senses for a time. The love of Radha is true eternal felicity, to which the mind of the repentant sinner at lust turns from the sensual and fleeting pleasures of this world. This may be the conception of the poet; and the following passage which we quote from

[10] 1. *mañjutara-kuñjatala-kelisadane*
praviśa rādhe mādhava-samīpam iha vilasa|
rati-rabhasa-hasita-vadane||

2. *nava bhavad-aśoka-dala-śayana-sāre*
praviśa rādhe mādhava-samīpam iha vilasu|
kuca-kalasa-tarala-hāre||

3. *kusuma-caya-racita-śuci-vāsa-gehe*
praviśa rādhe mādhava-samipam iha vilasa|
kusuma-sukumāra-dehe||

4. *mṛdu-cala-malaya-pavana-surabhi-śite*
praviśa rādhe mādhava-samīpam iha vilasa|
rasa-valita-lalita-gīte||

5. *vitata-bahu-valli-nava-pallava-ghane*
praviśa rādhe madhava-samīpam iha vilasa|
ciramalasapīna-joghane||

6. *madhu-mudita-madhupakula-kalitarave*
praviśa rādhe mādhava-samipam iha vilasa|
madana-rasa-sarasa-bhāve||

7. *madhuratara-pika-nikara-ninada-mukhare*
praviśa rādhe mādhava-samīpam iha vilasa|
daśana-ruci-rucira-śikhare||

—*Gita Govinda,* 11th *Sarga*

Sir Edwin Arnold's exquisite translation of *Gita Govinda* will shew that the five milkmaids, described by Jayadeva, in reality personify the five senses,—smell, sight, touch, taste, and hearing :

One with star blossomed champac wreathed, woos him to rest his head,
On the dark pillow of her breast so tenderly outspread ;
And o'er his brow with roses blown she fans a fragrance rare,
That falls on the enchanted sense like rain in thirsty air ;
While the company of damsels wave many and odorous spray,
And Krishna laughing, toying, sighs the soft spring away.

Another gazing in his face, sits wistfully apart.
Searching it with those looks of love that leap from heart to heart ;
Her eyes — afire with shy desire, veiled by their lashes black—
Speak so that Krishna cannot choose but send the message back ;
In the company of damsels whose bright eyes in the ring
Shine round him with soft meanings in the merry light of spring.

The third one of that dazzling band of dwellers in the wood—
Body and bosom panting with the pulse of youthful blood—
Leans over him, as in his ear a lightsome thing to speak,
And then with leaf-soft lip imprints a kiss below his cheek ;
A kiss that thrills, and Krishna turns at the silken touch
To give it back, — And Radha ! forgetting the too much.

And one with arch smile beckons him away from Jumna's banks,

Where the tall bamboos bristle like spears in battle ranks,
And plucks his cloth to make him come into the mango shade,
Where the fruit is ripe and golden, and the milk and cakes are laid;
Oh! golden red the mangoes, and glad the feasts of Spring,
And fair the flowers to lie upon and sweet the dancers sing.

Sweetest of all that Temptress who dances for him now
With subtle feet which part and meet in the Ras measure slow,
To the chime of silver bangles, and the beat of rose-leaf hands,
And pipe and lute and cymbal played by the wood-land bands;
So that wholly passion-laden—eye, ear, sense, soul o'ercome—
Krishna is theirs in the forest; his heart forgets its home.

It is likely, the whole poem, like Spenser's Fairy Queen, is meant to be an allegory; but the allegory is so overlaid with rich, vivid, and melodious descriptions, that the reader misses the allegory, does not care for the allegory, and pours on the descriptions. The fame of Jayadeva rests not on the philosophic or moral signification of the *Gita Govinda*, but on the spledid imagery, the tender feeling, and the melodious descriptions with which the work is replete.

In his own words, "whatever is delightful in the modes of music, whatever is exquisite in the sweet art of love, let the happy and wise learn from the song of Jayadeva."[11]

[11] *yad gandharvakulā sukauśalam anudhyānam cayadvaiṣṇavam*
yacchṛṅgāra-viveka tattva-racanā-kāvyeṣu lītāyitam|
tat-sarvam jayadeva-paṇḍita-kaveḥ kṛṣṇaikatānāt manaḥ
sānandāḥ pariśodhayantu sudhiyaḥ śrī-gīto-govindataḥ||

CHAPTER III

EARLY BENGALI LYRIC POETRY.—CHANDIDAS (FOURTEENTH CENTURY)

THE student who peruses with pleasure the polished works of Bankim Chandra or Madhusudan will scarcely suppose that the stream of Bengali literature, which has only in recent days attained such purity and expanse, began to flow as early as the fourteenth century of the Christian era[1]. And he will scarcely think that Chaucer of England and Chandidas[2] of Bengal were well nigh contemporaneous writers; that five hundred years have rolled away since Chandidas first wrote and sang; or, calculating twenty-five years to a generation, that twenty generations have chanted the lays and ditties of this Father of Bengali Lyric Poetry.

Chandidas is the earliest vernacular poet of Bengal,[3] but it is not possible to speak of him without saying something of Bidyapati, the earliest poet of Behar. Tradition has handed down the names of these two poets together: they

[1] See footnote 5, Ch. I—Ed.

[2] There is a great controversy about the identity and time of Caṇḍīdāsa. Some scholars believe that there were different persons of this name bearing the title Dvija, Dīna, Baḍu etc., while others are inclined to the view that there were two Caṇḍīdāsas of whom one preceded and the other followed Caitanya, the greatest exponent of Bengal Vaiṣṇavism; Caitanya is said to have enjoyed the songs of the former with great relish.

The so-called *Śrīkṛṣṇa-kīrtana,* discovered in the beginning of the present century, appears to have been composed by one Ananta Baḍu Caṇḍidāsa. It was composed, according to some eminent scholars, sometime between the 12th century and the 15th. *Śrīkṛṣṇa-kīrtana* is an assumed title, the manuscript on which the vulgate text is based containing no name of the work.

Stray *padas* of varying poetical merit pass current under the name of Caṇḍidāsa; but whether or not these are by one and the same hand is controversial.—Ed.

[3] The authors of the *Caryāpadas, found* in the *Bauddha Gān O Dohā,* are earlier than Caṇḍīdāsa.—Ed.

lived and wrote about the same time; and their poetry has the same theme, the loves of Radha and Krishna. Jayadeva popularized this theme in his inimitable Sanscrit work *Gita Govinda*, composed in the twelfth century; Bidyapati took up the subject and composed his songs in the vernacular of Behar in the fourteenth century; and it is probable that Chandidas was only an imitator of Bidyapati, and drew his inspiration from his contemporary of Behar. Thus the earliest Bengali poetry that is extant is indebted by the earliest poetry of Behar.

Bidyapati flourished in Behar in the fourteenth century.[4] The descendants of the poet still possess the village of Bapsi in Tirhut by virtue of a deed of gift from Siva Sinha to the poet, dated 293 of the era of Lakshman Sen, *i.e.*, 1400 A. D. In this document Bidyapati has been described as a *Sukabi* or a poet of merit, so that he must have made his mark before 1400. A still more important document is the *Panji* or annals of Tirhut. It is an authentic history of that District, and began to be written in 1248 Saka, *i.e.*, 1325 A. D. The *Panji* gives an account of Bidyapati who is described as the son of Ganapati, and a courtier of king Siva Sinha. Siva Sinha ascended the throne in 1369 Saka, *i.e.*, 1446 A. D., and must therefore have given away Bapsi to the poet during the life-time of his father who reigned no less than 61 years. We further learn from the *Panji* that Siva Sinha had three wives, Padmabati, Lakhima Devi and Biswa Devi, who after the death of their husband successively reigned for 18 months, 9 years and 12 years. Siva Sinha and Lakhima Devi find frequent mention in the songs of Bidyapati, and there can be no doubt that the poet lived about the close of the fourteenth century, and adorned the court of Siva Sinha and his father by whom his talents were recognized and richly rewarded.

The fame of Bidyapati as a poet had spread throughout Bengal at the time of Chaitanya, and Chaitanya in his early youth was edified with the poetry of Bidyapati and Chandidas.

"Glory to Jayadeva, the king and ornament of poets, and

[4] There were several poets bearing this name or title. The date of this Vidyāpati has not yet been fixed with absolute certainty. Some scholars think that he was alive in the first quarter of the 15th century A.D.—Ed.

to Bidyapati the source of sweetness; glory to Chandidas, for sweetness unequalled in the world, whose sweet and pure strains in prose and verse my Master Gaur Chandra (Chaitanya) relished with Sharup Rai."[5]

Again,

"The Great Master (Chaitanya) with Ramananda Sen sings and hears day and night the songs of Chandidas and Bidyapati, and the sweet Gita Govinda."[6]

We have said before that Lakhima Devi the queen of Siva Sinha is often spoken of in Bidyapati's poems. Tradition has it that the intimacy between the princess and the poet was closer than was altogether justifiable, and that Bidyapati's death was caused by this illicit love. We have no hesitation in rejecting these stories altogether as the invention of later days.

We now return to Chandidas the subject of the present chapter. Chandidas was a native of the village of Nannur, in the District of Birbhum, about 24 miles to the east of Suri, and was a Brahman by caste. That he was contemporaneous with Bidyapati is sufficiently proved by several poems which have come to us, of which the following is the most noted:

"Chandidas heard of Bidyapati's merits, and became anxious to see him. Bidyapati heard of Chandidas's merits, and became anxious to see him. Both became curious. Bidyapati went off with Rup Narain alone for his companion. Chandidas too could not stay, but went off to see Bidyapati. In the way both sang each other's praise, and their hearts remained anxious for each other. Suddenly they met each other, but neither recognized the other. They knew each other when they heard their names."[7]

[5] *jaya jayadeva kavi nṛpati śiromaṇi vidyāpati rasa-dhām|*
jaya jaya caṇḍīdās rasa-śekhara akhil bhuvane anupam||
cakara-racita madhura-rasa niramala gadya-padyamaya gīt
prabhu mor gauracandra āsvādilā rāy svarūpa-sahit||

[6] *caṇḍīdas vidyāpati, rāyer nāṭak gīt,*
karṇāmṛta śrī-gīta-govinda|
svarūp rāmānanda sane, mahāprabha ratri dine,
gān sune param ānanda||

[7] *caṇḍīdās śuni vidyāpati-guṇa daraśane bhela anurāg|*
vidyāpati suni caṇḍidāsa-guṇa daraśane bhelo anurāg||
duhu utkaṇṭhita bhela|

The traditions current about the life of Chandidas give us some clue to the nature of the rivalry which has ever existed in Bengal between the Vaishnava and Sakta creeds. Chandidas, as his name implies, was by birth a Sakta, *i.e.*, a worshipper of Chandi, Durga or Sakti, as the goddess is variously called.

It is said that in his early youth, Chandidas worshipped an image of Sakti which was called Bishalakshmi, and the poet often addresses the goddess in his works. As may well be imagined, the conversion of Chandidas to Vaishnavism has given rise to many tales. It is said that, on a certain day, he saw a beautiful flower floating on the river where he had gone to bathe. He took it up and went to worship Bishalakshmi. The goddess appeared in person, and asked for the flower that she might place it on her head. The worshipper was awe-struck, and enquired what sronge virtue the flower could possess, so as to induce the goddess to appear in person, and to wish to keep it on her head, instead of allowing the poet to place it at her feet. The goddess replied, "Foolish child, my Master has been worshipped with that flower, it is not fit for my feet, let me hold it on my head." "And who may *thy* Master be?" enquired the poet. *Krishna,* was the reply; and from that day the poet exchanged the worship of the goddess for that of Krishna.

It is scarcely necessary to add, that later Vaishnava writers have taken advantage of Chandidas's conversion to prove the superiority of their deity, and have invented this fable. One thing however is plain, namely, that the rivalry between the two creeds has prevailed in Bengal, as elsewhere in India, from remote times.

Chandidas has immortalized the washerwoman Rami in his poems, and numerous are the stories told about their loves. The poet was informed that he could not perform *Sadhan*

saṅgahi rūpanārāyaṇa kevala vidyāpati cali gela||
caṇḍidās tav rahai nā pārai, calala daraśana lāgi |
pantha hi duhū jana, duhū guna gāota,
duhū hiye duhū rahū jāgi ||
daivahi duhū dohā daraśana pāola, lakhai na pārai koi
duhū dohā nāma śravaṇe tehi jānala,
rūpanārāyaṇa goi|| —*Pada Kalpataru*

till he had a fair companion, not by marriage, not for money, but one to whom his heart would be spontaneously drawn at the first sight. Our poet went out in search of such a person, and it was not long before he found one. A washerwoman was washing clothes on the river side, the poet saw her and was fascinated. Day after day he would go to the river side with a fishing rod as a pretext, and sat there, gazing on the woman. Words followed and love ensued, and the poet left his home and parents, and ever afterwards lived with Rami, a washer-woman as she was by caste.

Chandidas was a renowned singer. One day, it is said, he went to a neighbouring village Matipur to sing with his paramour; and when they were returning, the house in which they had taken shelter fell down, and they were both crushed and died in each other's arms. The story has perhaps little foundation in fact. We now turn to the works of these poets.

The poetry of Chandidas presents a striking contrast to that of Bidyapati. Both are poets of a high order, both sang of the amours of Krishna and Radha, both are noted for the beauty of their songs, but here the parallel ends. Bidyapati excels in the richness of his imagery, the wide range of his ideas, the skill and art displayed in his varied similes. Chandidas has but his native, simple, excessive sweetness in place of all these qualities. Bidyapati ransacks the unbounded stores of Nature and of Art to embellish his poetry; Chandidas looks within, and records the fond workings of a feeling, loving heart in simple strains. In Chandidas's poetry there is a wealth of feeling and pathos; Bidyapati combines this with a quick fancy, a varied imagery, a leaning for grace and ornament. The faults of the two poets are also characteristic. Chandidas is cloying, and sometimes monotonous Bidyapati is often artificial in his images and ideas. At the same time both display a knowledge of the workings of a lover's heart, and portray them feelingly and minutely,—the first troubled impressions of love, the resistless force of its influence, the bitter pangs of separation and jealousy, the workings of hope, the effects of despair.

We will try to illustrate our remarks with a few extracts. There is no English version of either Bidyapati or Chandidas, and we have therefore for our English readers ventured to render into English verse the extracts made from the poets. We need scarcely remark that our version will very often fail to convey the deep feeling which charactetrizes the original.

We make an extract at random from Bidyapati.[8] It describes the first impressions of love in the heart of Krishna on seeing Radha.

Soon did the lovely vision part!
'Tis gone! I wake with sudden start!
A cloud-wrapped lightning sent its dart
Upon this troubled love-sick heart.
Scarce half removed was her veil,
Upon her lips played half a smile,
And half a glance her sweet eyes shed,
And half her bosom was displayed,
The rest her *anchal* did conceal,—
I gazed and felt my senses reel !
Her beauty, bright as burnished gold,
Love's amorous robe did sweet enfold,
And flung love's soft and silken chain,
Upon the hearts of prostrate men!
Her pearly teeth were sweetly placed
On ruby lips with beauty graced,
And soft she spoke,—I gazed in vain,
Insatiate gazed on her again !

Our readers must be struck with the *art* of the poet, with the similes and figures with which the small poem is so beautifully embellished, we had almost said, so thickly crowded. In this Bidyapati is in his own element. Not so Chandidas. He has neither the power nor the inclination to rove. He feels deeply, and sings feelingly. We quote from his poems a converse passage, a passage in which Radha is suddenly struck

[8] *sajani bhāla kari pekhana nā bhela*|
meghamālā sange taḍita latā janu hṛdaye śel dei gela||
ādha ācala khasi, ādha vadane hāsi, ādhai nayana taraṅga |
ādha uraja heri, ādha ācara bhari, taba dhari dagadhe anaṅga ||
eke tanu gorā, kanaya kaṭorā, atanu kācala upām|
hari hari kaha man, janu bujhi aichana, phāsa pasārala kām||
daśana mukutā-pāti, adhara milāyata, mṛdu mṛdu kaha tāhi bhāṣā
vidyāpati kaha, ataye se duḥkha raha, heri heri nā puralo āśā ||

and entranced at hearing the very name of Krishna.[9] We translate it thus.

Friend! who hath named that name?
  Through me it steals.
  My heart it thrills,
My soul it doth inflame!
  Ah who shall tell
  What sweet doth dwell
In that beloved strain!
  I name that name,
  My soul's all flame!
Oh! will he come again?

We extract a somewhat longer piece[10] from Chandidas. It is a loving appeal from Radha to Krishna, and a more touching appeal it would be difficult to find anywhere.

Love! how shall I my feelings tell?
  Be mine, in death and life,
In after-lives, in future births,
  To be thy duteous wife.
Yes! to thy feet my heart be tied
  By silken ties of love,
I offer all, my heart and soul,
  I'll be your doating slave!

[9] *sai kevā śunāile śyām-nām,*
kāner bhitar diyā marame paśila go
ākul kariyā mor prāṇ ||
nā jāni katek madhu śyām nāme āche go
vadane chāḍite nāhi pāre ;
japite japite nām avalā karila go
kemane pāiva sai tāre||

[10] *vādhu ki ār valiva āmi* |
maraṇe jivane janame janame prāṇanātha haio tumi||
tomār caraṇe āmār parāṇe bādhila premer phāsi |
sav samapiyā ek man haiyā niścay hailām dāsi||
bhāviyā dekhilām e tin bhuvane ār keha mor āche|
rādhā vali keha sudhāite nāi dāḍāva kāhār kāche||
ekule okule gokule dukūle āpanā valiva kāy|
śītal valiyā śaraṇ lailām o duti komal pāy ||
nā ṭhela nā ṭhela chale avala akhale ye kay ucit tor|
bhāviyā dekhilām prāṇanātha vine gati ye nahika mor ||
ākhir nimiṣe yadi nāhi dekhi tave se parāṇe mari |
caṇḍīdāse kay paraś ratan galāy gāthiyā pari|

I've thought if in this wide wide world
  Another friend I own,
In loving voice to name my name.
  Alas! alas! there's none!
In earth, in heaven, in after-world,
  Alas! who loveth me?
O! to thy feet I turn for help.
  To thee alone! to thee!
Then do not spurn me, I am weak,
  O! do not turn away
I've thought and felt, without thy help,
  I have no other way.
If for a moment thee I miss,
  A death-like trance I own;
I'll keep and nurse thee on my heart
  E'en as a precious stone!

The same intense feeling,—the same absence of all figures of speech, marks this poem. We shall pass on to another extract,[11] describing the despair of Radha in the absence of her beloved.

A cruel throb is in my heart!
  I'll leave my home,
  And thither roam,
Where never's known love's fatal art.

Friend! who shall say that love is sweet?
  I loved, and smiled,
  My heart's beguiled,
And life-long sorrow is my fate!

For love should e'er a damsel sigh,
  O! spare her shame,

[11] *ki dāruṇ buker vyathā |*
se deśe jāiva ye deśe nā śuni pāp piriter kathā ||
sai ke vale piriti bhāla |
hāsite hāsite piriti kariyā kāndite janam gela ||
kulavatī haiyā kule dāḍāñā ye dhanī piriti kare |
tuṣer anal yena sājāiyā emati puḍiyā mare ||
hām vinodinī e duḥkhe duḥkhinī preme chala chala ākhi |
caṇḍīdas kahe se gati haiyā parāṇ saṁśay dekhi ||

In fire and flame,
A kinder death, O let her die!

For I have felt this bitter grief,
My eye-balls shine
With ceaseless brine,
Says Chandidas, O for her life!

Seldom doth Bidyapati manifest such deep feeling and pathos. His strong point lies, as we have already said, in his imagery and embellishments. But nevertheless the poet of Behar too can equal the poet of Bengal in his own element when he chooses to divest himself of his art, and sings as only a true poet can sing; and the celebrated lines quoted below[12] are an instance to the point.

I've gazed and gazed on beauty's glow,
E'er since my life began,
Insatiate still my eye-balls swim,
Fain would I gaze again!
I've heard his honey-dropping words,
E'er since my life began,
Insatiate still my ear remains,
Fain would I hear again!
What happy nights with him I passed,
Unhappy yet I feel,
What years my heart I cooled on his,
Insatiate burns it still.

Over a hundred years elapsed between the time of Chandidas and that of Chaitanya. Within these hundred years a host of poets of lesser note flourished. A large number of poems composed within this period are ascribed to Govinda Das. It is easy to perceive therefore that more than one poet of that name flourished. Indeed *Govinda Das* means servant of Krishna, and it is not unlikely that most of the poets who wrote about the loves of that deity assumed that coveted name,

[12] *janam avadhi hām rūpa nihāranu nayana nā tirapita bhela* |
soi madhura bol śravaṇahi śunalu śrutipathe paraśana gela ||
kata madhu-yāminī rabhase goyāinu nā bujhinu kaichana kela |
lākha lākha yuga hiye hiye rākhanu tabu hiyā juḍana nā gela ||

Balaram Das, Jnan Das, and many other poets of lesser note, flourished during that period.

Their poetry or rather song has the same characteristic qualities. They are always sweet, and often display a vivid fancy and considerable depth of feeling, and they all relate to the amours of Radha and Krishna. We have examined the merits of the best poets of the class, and we think it unnecessary to go over the entire field. There is a tolerably good collection of their works in the *Pada Kalpataru,* and it is by no means a waste of time to go over these old authors, even from a literary point of view. The admires of modern Bengali litetrature will be surprised at the sweetness and beauty that pervade these old compositions. That they have been preserved so long and so carefully is owing to the Vaishnavas, and to them, therefore, Bengal owes an immense debt of gratitude.

CHAPTER IV

KASIRAM DAS AND HIS MAHABHARATA (FIFTEENTH CENTURY)

IN the last Chaptetr we have spoken of the lyric poetry of the fourteenth century. It was probably in the fifteenth century[1] that Kasiram Das undertook and performed the mighty task of translating[2] the Sanscrit epic *Mahabharata* into Bengali verse. Kasiram's work is the first great and national literary work in the Bengali language, it is a foundation of rock on which the national literature of Bengal has been subsequently built up. Chandidas is the *Father of Bengali song;* Kasiram Das is the *Father of Bengali literature,* properly so called.

Unfortunately we know little of the life of this great poet. He was born in Singi, near Katwa in the District of Burdwan; and the supposed site of his house is still pointed out as *Keser Bhita.* He was a Kayastha by caste, and his bold endeavour to popularise the great epic of ancient India among his countrymen in simple Bengali verse was regarded with suspicion and distrust. A Brahman poet *Krittibas* followed his example, and translated the other great epic Ramayana into Bengali verse, and his laudable work too was viewed with jealousy and displeasure. And a popular verse is often repeated:—

kaśīdese kṛttivese, ār bāmunghese,
ei tin sarvaneśe|

"Kasidas and Krittibas, and those who constantly seek to associate with Brahmans ;—these are dangerous men."

Such narrow jealousy however does not turn the tide of knowledge, and the great poet of the fifteenth century first

[1] According to Sukumar Sen, he was born towards the end of the sixteenth century, and probably composed his work in the first decade of the seventeenth. (vide *Vāṅgālā Sāhityer Itihās*, 1948, I, pp. 456 and 461).—Ed.

[2] Strictly speaking, Kāśīrām's work is not a translation, but an adaptation as the author himself states below.—Ed.

led his countrymen into that store-house of Sanscrit poetry and learning which we have learnt to appreciate more and more with the lapse of centuries and the increase of knowledge.

The main story of the *Mahabharata* is well known. It describes the contest between the Pandavas and the Kuru princes for the throne of Kuruland. The Pandavas were banished at first, but they made powerful friends and demanded their share, and the western portion of Kuruland, with Indraprastha for its capital, was ceded to them. They staked and lost this kingdom however at dice, and retired into the wilderness, according to their plighted word. On the expiry of the prescribed period they came forward again and demanded a share of the kingdom. The Kuru princes refused this,—and the consequence was a disastrous battle in which all the great princes of Northern India took part, and in which the Kuru tribe was well nigh exterminated. The Pandavas won, and established their rule in the Kuru kingdom.

Connected with the main story, the manners and customs of the times, the pomp and splendour of courts, the rules of war and peace, the power and jealousies of kings, and the heroism and chivalry of the Kshatriya warriors of ancient India have been described with graphic force, and unsurpassed power. On the other hand, the inner workings of the human mind and all its varied feelings, love, hatred, jealously between rival princes, revenge that knew no satiety, the patience of a suffering saint, the greatness of a true hero;—all the various shades of human character, from the sublime virtues of Bhishma who drew forth tears of admiration from the enemies who killed him, to the fiery jealousies of Duryodhana who engaged the whole of northern India in a disastrous war rather than cede five villages to his much-hated cousins,—all that a true poet and a great poet is capable of, has been worked out with pencil of a Homer. Homer's characters are not more life-like than the men of flesh and blood, of determination and valour, who figure in the great Sanscrit epic; and Homer's incidents are not more sublime in conception or graphic in description than those of the Mahabharata. The world has seen no nobler creation of the imagination than the great epic of the Hindus.

But while the epic of Homer was collected and preserved by Pisistratus the ruler of Athens, as early as the sixth century before Christ, no Hindu ruler of antiquity took the trouble of preserving the great Hindu epic from subsequent additions and intèrpolations. Generations of poets have accordingly added to the old epic until it has almost changed its character, and the crystal stream of true epic poetry is lost in a wide morass of mythical episodes and mythological stories, of cosmogony and theogony, of never-ending didactic and dogmatic instructions. All this episodical matter fills three-fourths of the epic in its present shape ; the leading narrative barely takes up a fourth part.

When the evil had been done, an attempt was made to prevent further expansion of the work. The contents of the epic described in a sort of preface, and the number of *slokas* or couplets in each Book was given, so as to present further addition. The curious reader will find these numbers in the note given below, as well as the number of couplets actually found in the published edition of the work.

Books.	*Sections.*	*Number of couplets according to preface.*	*Number of couplets in the Asiatic Society's Edition*
Adi	227	8884	8479
Sabha	78	2511	2709
Vana	269	11664	17478
Virata	67	2050	2376
Udyoga	186	6698	7656
Bhishma	117	5884	5656
Drona	170	8909	9650
Karna	69	4964	5046
Salya	59	3220	3671
Sauptika	18	870	811
Stri	27	775	827
Santi	339	14732	13943
Anusasana	146	8000	7796
Asvamedha	103	3320	2900
Asramavasa	42	1506	1105
Mausala	8	320	292
Mahaprasthana	3	320	109
Sarga	5	209	312
	1,933	84,836	90,816

In recent years, the *Mahābhārata* has been edited, according to

The total number of couplets enumerated in the preface comes to near eighty-five thousand. But the limit so fixed has been exceeded in still later ages, further additions have been made, and the Sanscrit *Mahabharata* now published contains over ninety thousand couplets, excluding the *Harivansa*. It is an encyclopædic work; all the tales and traditions and mythological stories of India have been comprehended in this one work. As a store-house of Hindu traditions, it has thus been rendered unique and invaluable; as an epic poem it has been ruined.

Endeavours have been made from time to time to disentangle the leading narrative from episodical matter, and to publish it separately. But as yet, such endeavours have not met with success.[3]

In undertaking to translate this vast work into Bengali verse for Bengali readers, Kasiram Das very wisely decided to condense the matter in the translation.[4] The Bengali version is a little over one-third of the original Sanscrit poem in extent, consisting of about thirty-six thousand couplets. The work of condensing the original epic has been performed with thoughtful care; and while mere verbal descriptions have been greatly abridged, the stories and incidents have been repeated in the Bengali version with scarcely any important omission.

One instance, selected at random, will convey to our readers the process adopted by the translator. The famous story of Sakuntala has been told in the original *Mahabharata* in six sections of the First Book, *viz.* sections LXIX to LXXIV. Section LXIX, giving an account of Dushyanta's hunt in thirty-one couplets, has been reduced to eight couplets by Kasiram. Section LXX, describing king Dushyanta's entry into Kanva's

scientific principles, by the Bhandarkar Oriental Research Institute, Poona. The edition, with Bengali translation of the epic, by Haridās Siddhāntavāgīśa is a noteworthy work.—Ed.

[3] The edition of the great epic published by the Asiatic Society of Bengal is well known to all scholars. A meritorious translation in Bengali prose by the late munificent Kali Prasanna Sinha is the version now in general use in Bengal. An English translation of the work was undertaken and nearly completed by the late Pratap Chandra Roy. His widow has piously undertaken to complete this work.

[4] *See* page 32.

forest in fifty couplets, has been reduced to ten couplets in Bengali. Section LXXI, narrating Dushyanta's meeting and conversation with Sakuntala, has been reduced from forty-two couplets in the original to twenty-five in the translation. Section LXXII concludes Sakuntala's story of her birth in nineteen couplets in Sanscrit, and has been rendered in nineteen couplets by Kasiram. Section LXXIII speaks of Dushyanta's marriage with Sakuntala in thirty-three couplets, which have been rendered in twenty-four in Bengali. And section LXXIV narrates the subsequent story of Sakuntala and of the birth of Bharata in one hundred thirty-eight couples, which have been translated in eighty-six in the Bengali version. We reproduce below the whole[5] of section LXXII with Kasiram's version, and the reader will find

[5] For consideration of space, we reproduce only a part :—Ed.

Adiparvan—Ch. 72

Kaṇva uvāca :

evamuktastayā śakraḥ saṁdideśa sadāgatim|
pratiṣṭhata tadā kāle menakā vāyunā saha||
athāpaśyat varārohā tapasā dagdha-kilviṣam|
viśvāmitram tapyamānam menakā bhīrurāśrame||
abhivādya tataḥ sā tam prākriḍat ṛṣi-sannidhau|
apovāha ca vāso'syā mārutaḥ śaśi-sannibham ||

* * * *

tasyā rūpaguṇān dṛṣṭvā sa tu viprarṣabhastadā|
cakāra bhāvam samsargāt tayā kāmavaśam gataḥ||

* * * *

Śakuntalā uvāca :

* * * *

kaṇvam hi pitaram manye pitaram svam ajānatī |
iti te kathitam rājan yathā vṛttam śrutam mayā||

Sakuntalār janma-kathā :

indra ājñā kaila saṅge yāha duijan|
devarāj ājñā pāiyā calila takhan||
henamate save gela munir gocar|
muni dekhi menakār kāmpila antar ||
atiśay suveśā haiyā vidyādhari|
munir nikaṭe krīḍā kare māyā kari||
henakāle vāyu vahe ati kharatar|
uḍāiya vastra tār phelila antar||

* * * *

e sakal kautuk dekhila munivar|
śarīrete bhedila kāmer pañcaśar||

* * * *

gṛhe āni pālan karila munivar|
teñi āmi tār kanyā śuna daṇḍadhar||

that Kasiram can be a faithful translator when he is not called upon to condense the matter. Occasionally, however, a wide divergence is noticeable between the original and the translation, and in some places an additional section or story is found in the translation which does not occur in the original. The excellent story of Sribatsa, for instance, which Krishna narrates to Yudhishthira in an early part of *Vana Parva* in the Bengali translation, does not occur in the corresponding portion of the original, as published by the Asiatic Society of Bengal.

Such is the method in which Kasiram Das has performed the great task which he imposed upon himself. The mere mechanical work of translating and condensing a great Sanscrit epic into over thirty-six thousand Bengali couplets is a tremendous task. If we suppose that Kasiram composed fifteen couplets every day, and that he worked twenty days in every month, he must have laboured ten years of his life to bring this great work to completion.

And the merits of the translation are not of a mean order. The reader must not look for the heroic spirit and the epic grandeur of the original in the Bengali version; but in simplicity, sweetness and fluency, in a lucid flow of narration and an inexhaustible flow of verse, Kasiram Das remains unsurpassed and unequalled in Bengali literature.

And if success be a proof of true merit, Kasiram's merit is beyond praise. No work in Bengali, scarcely even the Ramayana of Krittibas, is more extensively read and more deeply honoured by the people of Bengal, specially of the upper classes. The endless traditions and tales of the past times have a charm and an attracion, the morals inclucated and the incidents narrated never fail to please, and the translator's dignified, but simple and graceful verse never tires. Mothers know no better theme for imparting moral instruction to their daughters, wives know no better work for whiling away an idle hour, and elderly men know no rich store from which to narrate stories to groups of little children night after night. Thus the tales of the *Mahabharata* have been handed down from generation to generation with never-failing interest, and where is the Bengali who has not in his boyish days passed many a long winter evening over these moral tales which can never, never be other than interesting and instructive ?

CHAPTER V

KRITTIBAS AND HIS RAMAYANA (FIFTEENTH CENTURY)

THERE are reasons to believe that Kasiram Das translated the *Mahabharata* in the fifteenth century.[1] Krittibas's date is very uncertain; but it is probable that he produced his Bengali version of the *Ramayana* probably about the close of the same century.

Of the life of Krittibas we know as little as we know of Kasiram Das, except that he was a Brahman by caste, and was born at Fulia, near Santipur, in the District of Nadia. The two great pioneers of Bengali poetry lived in the opposite shores of the sacred Bhagirathi.

The task which Krittibas set before himself was less arduous than what his predecessor Kasiram had performed. The *Ramayana* in the original Sanscrit is not encyclopædic in its character; its main story about the life and adventures of Rama is not overgrown with mythology, cosmogony and theogony; its episodes are rare and restricted to the early portion of the work; and its leading narrative is seldom interrupted. The *Ramayana* in fact is mainly the work of a single poet,[2] working

[1] See Ch. IV. f.n. 1.—Ed.

[2] It cannot be denied that it has undergone alterations through succeeding centuries, but in spite of them the epic poem continues to be one connected story, mainly the creation of one mind. A learned writer in the *Westminster Review* writes :—"The poem has evidently undergone considerable alteration since the time of its first composition, but still, underneath all the subsequent additions, the original elements are preserved, and careful criticism might perhaps separate the interpolations, and present the more genuine parts as a whole by themselves. The task however, would be difficult, and perhaps as impracticable as it has proved in the Homeric poems. For many ages it is certain that the work existed only by oral tradition, and each rhapsodist added or altered at his pleasure, or to suit the taste or vanity of the princely family whom he served. The measure of the poem, moreover, is of a somewhat fatal facility, and many rhapsodists would naturally be ambitious of mingling their own songs with those of their bards, and the habit of repetition would at once supply them with a vocabulary of epic phrases to suit their purpose. Whole chapters thus

out a single connected story; whereas the *Mahabharata* is a creation of many centuries, and a storehouse of endless stories. The *Ramayana* contains professedly twenty-four thousand couplets or epic verses; the *Mahabharata* contains professedly eighty-five thousand.. The translator of the *Ramayana* had therefore a lighter task to perform than the translator of the *Mahabharata*.

In undertaking this task, Krittibas, like his great predecessor Kasiram Das, wisely determined to condense the original. We do not exactly know the length of Krittibas's version, for, as we will state hereafter, that version has been considerably altered and added to by mischievous editors in recent times. An edition of the work, printed in 1803 in the Serampur Mission Press, has however been reprinted; and from this edition we find that the twenty-four thousand couplets of the original work have been condensed into about sixteen thousand Bengali couplets.

But Krittibas has gone father than this. A comparison of his *Ramayana** with the original shews that his version is no translation at all, but merely a new narration of the story of the ancient epic in his own way. There is considerable divergence in the arrangement of the matter; much of the contents in the original has been omitted, and many new incidents and stories have been introduced. And even when we compare the accounts of the same incidents in the two works, we find

betray their origin by their barrenness of thought and laborious mimicry of the epic spirit, which in the case of the old poets had spontaneously burst out of the heart's fulness like the free song of a child. But when the Indian Pisistratus arose who collected these separate songs and reduced them to their present shape, the genuine and spurious were alike included, and no Hindu critic ever appears to have attempted to discriminate between them."—*Westminster Review*, Vol. L.

An edition of the Sanscrit *Ramayana* (Bengal Recension) with an Italian translation was prepared by Gorresio, and published at the expense of the late king of Sardinia. A French translation has been given to the world by the indefatigable Hippolyte Fanche, and for a very meritorious metrical translation into English we are indebted to Ralph Griffith. Pandit Hem Chandra Vidyaratna has conferred a lasting obligation on the people of Bengal by publishing an edition of the Sanscrit work (North-west Recension) with an excellent translation in prose; and the late poet Raj Krishna Rai has given us a faithful and commendable translation of the great work in Bengali verse.

them so dissimilar that the Bengali work cannot be called a condensed translation of the Sanscrit work.

One instance will illustrate this. The breaking of Janaka's bow by Rama, and the nuptials of Rama and his brothers, and the defeat of Parasurama, have been described in the last eleven sections of the First Book of the Sanscrit *Ramayana, viz.* sections LXVII to LXXVII, comprising 305 couplets. These subjects has been reproduced in Krittibas's work (reprint of edition of 1803) in one long section of 365 couplets, but it is not possible to call this section a translation, in any sense, of the eleven sections of the Sanscrit work. The story has been differently told in the two works; and Krittibas narrates the events entirely in his own way, without any reference whatever to the Sanscrit work.[3]

[3] We quote the account of Rama's marriage from the two works. The Bengali poet describes a Bengali marriage ceremony of the present day !

(Editor's note : For consideration of space, we retain only some typical verses and omit the others quoted by the author).

Bāla-kāṇḍa : Canto 73.

tataḥ sītām samānīya sarvābharaṇa-bhūṣitām |
samakṣamagneḥ saṃsthāpya rāghavābhimukhe tadā ||
abravīd janako rājā kauśalyānanda-vardhanam |
iyam sītā mama sūtā sahadharmacarī tava ||
pratīccha caināṃ bhadram te pāṇim gṛhṇīṣva pāṇinā |
pativratā mahābhāgā chāyevānugatā sadā ||
ityuktvā prākṣipad rājā mantrapūtam jalam tadā |
sādhu sādhviti devānām ṛṣīṇām vadatām tadā |
devadundubhi-nirghoṣaḥ puṣpa-varṣo mahān abhūt ||

* * * *

Jānakīr vivāha-kathā :

galāy vastra diyā bale janak rājan |
tomār putre kanyā diyā lailām śaraṇ ||

* * * *

kanyā āna āna bale yata bandhu-gaṇ |
nānā veś bhūṣā karen yata sakhī-gaṇe |

* * * *

māthāy keha keha dey āmalakī |
tolā jale snān eve kare candramukhī ||

* * * *

kapāle tuliyā dila nirmal sindūr |

* * * *

dui bāhu śaṅkhe paren ati vilakṣaṇ |
śaṅkher upar vāje soṇār kaṅkaṇ ||

* * * *

The Sixth Book of the epic describes the war between Rama and Ravana, which is the crowning incident of the story; and in describing this war Krittibas has scarcely followed the story of the Sanscrit work. The first forty sections of this Book in the original Sanscrit, comprising about a thousand couplets, have been omitted by Krittibas, and he substitutes a small part of this story in his first five sections. The war commences with the sending of Angada as an envoy to Ravana, which is described in Section XLI of the Sanscrit work, and in Section VI of Krittibas.

The incidents of the war then follow generally in the same order as in Sanscrit. But Krittibas's account of the battles is his own, and he has introduced some new incidents and new warriors of which there is no mention in the Sanscrit. The account of Mahi-Ravana and Ahi-Ravana and the childish episode of Hanuman carrying the solar orb under his arm find no mention in the Sanskrit epic.

It will thus appear that Krittibas's work is not a translation of the Sanscrit work. A class of reciters called *Kathakas* have flourished in this country from olden times; they recite sacred legends before large audiences; they amuse and entertain their hearers by their wit, or move them to tears by their eloquence; and they thus teach the unlettered public in the traditions of the past, and preserve from age to age the literary heritage of the nation. The *Ramayana* is a fit subject for *Kathakas;* and the recitation lasts for a month or more, the speaker taking up the story every day from the point where he left it on the preceding day. It is supposed with reason that Krittibas learnt the story of the *Ramayana* from *Kaṭhakas*, and that without attempting to translate the Sanscri epic he has

suvarṇa āsane vasilen rūpavatī|
cāri dike jvāli dila sohāger vātī||

* * * *

strīlokerā parihās kare seiṭhāye|
keha bale hāte dhara keha bale pāye||

* * * *

kanyā dān kare rājā vividha prakāre|
pañca haritakī diyā parihār kare||

* * * *

vāsar ghar sājāila yata sakhīgan|
rām sītā vāsar ghare vañcila duijan||

given his version of the story as he heard it. The poet has himself told us in several places in his work that he has composed it *as he heard it recited.*

But if Krittibas fails us as a translator, as a poet and composer he rises in our estimation. He narration is fluent and easy and often sparkles with the richest humour. Kasiram Das is a pious and learned student who has endeavoured to give his countrymen a condensed translation of the Sanscrit *Mohabharata;* Krittibas is a sprightly story-teller who tells the story of the *Ramayana* with his own native wit. Kasiram Das is anxious to teach his countrymen in the sacred traditions, the undying legends, and the didactic narrations, which compose the bulk of the *Mahabharata.* Krittibas delights in depicting in vivid colours the deeds of Hanuman, the fierce rage of the Rakshasas, the marvellous prowess of the god-like Rama. Kasiram Das approaches his subject with reverence, and writes in a chaste and dignified though simple style; Krittibas delights in the somewhat primitive battles between monkeys and giants, colours his description with his wit, and writes in the style of ordinary villagers. Kasiram Das's work is the favourite study of pious Hindu ladies and of religious and elderly men of the upper classes; Krittibas appeals more effectively to the million. The village *Mudi* (confectioner) reads his *Ramayana,* when waiting for his customers, and the village *Kalu* (oil-manufacturer) chants the story of Rama and Sita, as his bullock turns his primitive oil-mill with a slow creaking sound. To the upper ten-thousand, Kasiram Das's work is a repository of all the sacred traditions and moral lessons of the Hindus; to the class of vendors, shopkeepers and the like, as well as to the upper classes, Krittibas's work is a joy which endureth for work. For the millions of Bengal, the two works have been a means of moral education the value of which cannot be over-estimated.

The simplicity of Krittibas's style and the great circulation of his work among the lower as well as upper classes has led to the frequent tampering of his text by successive editors, until the editions now sold in the Bazars have ceased to be Krittibas's work. We have made our extracts from a reprint of the edition of 1803, as it is less corrupt than more recent editions; but even that edition is not absolutely correct. Pandit

Ramgati Nyaparatna has given us a passage from a manuscript of Krittibas's work written in 1099 of the Bengali Era, corresponding to 1693 of the Christian Era, and therefore two centuries old. We quote a passage below from this edition of 1693, as well as the corresponding passage from the edition of 1803, and from an ordinary Bazar edition of 1893.[4]

A comparison of the three passages quoted below will indicate the nature of the alterations which Krittibas's text has undergone within the last two hundred years. We may assume that the text of 1693 was what Krittibas wrote, as there was little of mischievous editorial activity before that date, and printing was unknown in Bengal. The alterations made between 1693 and 1803 are of a verbal nature, and however much they may be regretted, they are slight in comparison with what followed. In the absence of any more correct edition, we may accept the edition of 1803 as Krittibas's work for the purposes of criticism, and we thank the Gupta Press for giving us a reprint of this first printed edition of the work. Since 1803, however, printed editions of the work have multiplied, and the mischievous activity of editors has increased. The

[4] *tārā bale rām tumi janmilā uttam kule|*
āmār pati kāṭilā tumi pāiyā kon chale||
dekhā dekhi yujhite yadi bujhite pratāp|
ādekhā mārile prabhu baḍa pāinu tāp||
prabhu mor śāp nā dilen karuṇ hṛday |
muni śāp diva yena hay ṭa niścay||

—*Edition of* 1693

* * * *

tārā bale dhārmik tumi janma uttam kule|
āmār svāmike māra paiyā kona chale||
dekhā dekhi mārite yadi dekhite pratāp|
adekhā ghāy mārile prabhu pāilām tāp ||
prabhu śāp nāhi dilen karuṇ hṛday|
āmi śāp diva tomā phalibe niścay||

* * * *

—*Ed. of* 1893 (*Reprint*)

tārā bale rām tava janma raghukule|
āmār svāmike kena vināśile chale||
sammukhe mārite yadi dekhite pratāp|
lukāiyā mārile pāilām baḍa tāp||
śrīrām tomāre save bale dayāvān|
bhāla dekhāile āji tāhār pramāṇ||

—*Cal. Ed.* 1893

late Pandit Jai Gopal of the Sanscrit College is reputed to have recast the older editions and to have produced the modern ones. Comparing the text of 1803 with that of 1893 we find that the somewhat loose metre of Krittibas has been rectified, the number of syllables has been adjusted, the expressive but homely words of the poet have been replaced by more refined expressions, some lines have been added and thrown in here and there, and the homely beauty of Krittibas's poetry has been lost. To our ear, Krittibas's irregular verse and loose metre have more true music and more genial force in them than the corrected metre, the sanscritized expressions, and the more prolonged descriptions in the later editions of his work.

The Gupta Press has performed a patriotic work by reprinting the edition of 1803. But the task of producing an absolutely correct text of he work, from the old manuscripts still available, has yet to be done. The *Bangiya Sahitya Parishad* (Academy of Bengali Literature) has undertaken the task; and it will earn the gratitude of our countrymen by giving them a correct text of the immortal work of one of the earliest and greatest poets of Bengal.

Kasiram Das's work is perhaps less popular than that of Krittibas, and has been tampered with to a less extent. The great bulk of the work also, made further additions inadvisable even to modern editors, and the more dignified nature of the style and the subject rendered such additions by no means an easy task. But nevertheless verbal alterations have been made, as can be found out by comparison of a modern copy with an old manuscript. And the *Parishad* will perform a patriotic task by editing a correct edition of this work also.

The Bengali *Mahabhbarata* and *Ramayana* are the first great literary works in the Bengali language; they are the foundations on which Bengali literature is built. And the people of modern Bengal will not rest content till they get back these great works in their integrity.

CHAPTER VI

CHAITANYA AND HIS RELIGIOUS REFORMS (SIXTEENTH CENTURY)

WE have seen in the last two chapters that literary activity began in Bengal in the fourteenth and fifteenth centuries.[1] The Sixteenth century witnessed a great religious reform and a marked progress in philosophy and culture. Indeed similar movements were observable in every province of India in this age of renaissance and reform, which corresponds curiously with the age of renaissance and reform in Europe. It was in the fifteenth and sixteenth centuries that Kabir preached religious reform in southern and northern India, that Chaitanya preached and worked in Bengal, and the great Nanak founded a reformed religion in the Punjab. It was in this age that Kasiram and Krittibas translated the ancient epics into Bengali, and they were immediately followed by the great Sridhar who translated the epics into Marathi, and by the equally great Tulsi Das who rendered the Ramayana into Hindi. It was in this age or shortly after, that Mukundaram in Bengal, and Tukaram in Bombay, distinguished themselves by original compositions which are still dear to their countrymen. And it was in this age also that Raghunandan compiled a religious code for the Hindus of Bengal, and Raghunath started the school of philosophy which still attracts scores of students from all parts of India to the sacred precincts of Nadiya. The movements of the human mind are more widespread and far-reaching than historians generally suspect, and there are special eras of culture when the human mind all over the civilized world seems to expand under a vivifying influence, and moves onwards with a fresh vigour towards higher results. Such an era was the fifteenth and sixteenth centuries which produced men like Copernicus, Columbus and Luther in Europe; and such another era began in the eighteenth century which witnessed the Independ-

[1] See f.n. 3, Ch. I—Ed.

ence of America and the French Revolution. Chaitanya was the most remarkable product of the sixteenth century enlightenment in Bengal, and to a narration of his life and work we now address ourselves. His biographers, Krishna Das, Vrindavan Das and Lochan Das, have left us copious accounts of the life and work of their greater master, and though. as staunch Vaishnavas, they believed Chaitanya to be an incarnation of Krishna and have ascribed to him numberless miracles, yet it is not a difficult or a profitless task to glean from their accounts the real facts connected with the life of the great reformer of the sixteenth century.

About the middle of the 15th century, Upendra Misra, a wealthy and learned Vaishnava, lived in Sylhet. . He had seven sons of whom Jagannath Misra migrated to the town of Nabadwip or Nadiya. He had eight daughters by his wife Sachi, but none of them lived long. At last Sachi bore him two sons; the elder was named Viswarup, and the younger was the future reformer of Bengal.

He was born in Nabadwip in the year 1485 A. D.,[2] that is about the time when the great Luther was born in Europe. The women of the family and the neighbourhood came to see and bless the infant, and named it Nimai, and notwithstanding that the learned men of the locality gave the child the more pompous name of Viswambhar, Nimai the child was called by all who knew him. Later in life he was called Gauranga, or the fair-complexioned, Krishna Chaitanya, or the incarnation of Krishna, and sometimes Gaur Hari, or the fair Krishna,—Chaitanya being of a very fair complexion. while Krishna, whose incarnation he was supposed to be, was dark. Chaitanya is said to have been born in the evening when there was an eclipse of the moon, and his poetic biographer explains the circumstances by arguing that there was no need for a spotted moon in the sky, when an unspotted moon had appeared on earth !

Various are the anecdotes recounted of the infancy and boyhood of Chaitanya, all tending to shew that he was an iincarnate deity. While yet an infant "puking and mewling

[2] 1486, according to S. K. De (Vide his *Early History of the Vaisnava Faith* etc., 1942, p. 51).—Ed.

in its month's arm," Chaitanya seems to have been very troublesome, and to have never ceased crying, till the word *Hari* was shouted by the people around him, thus causing the name of Krishna to be preached and proclaimed before the infant had yet learnt to speak. On one occasion the little child was licking an earthen toy, when Sachi came in, and reproved him for mistaking earth for food. "And what is food but earth and dust?" argued the lisping boy, "and what is our body but dust?" A restless and mischievous boy as he was, he teased the girls of the neighbourhood and quarrelled with other boys. When the girls came to the river-side with rice and other things to worship images, the little truant appropriated the food to his own use, and bade them worship him, for *he* was the great Master of the gods and goddesses they had come to worship. Flying from his enraged mother the little boy one day hid himself in an unclean vessel. This provoked Sachi who bade him instantly to go and bathe in the Ganga (Hugli River) to purify himself. The young sage however calmly replied that uncleanliness dwelt not in outward things but in the mind. It may be easily imagined these and other anecdotes of a similar nature have been invented by the followers of Chaitanya to prove the godhead of their great master.

Chaitanya commenced his studies with Ganga Das Pandit and shewed great intelligence and aptitude for learning. It was about this time that the parents of Chaitanya began to think of a suitable match for his elder brother Viswarup, who was then in his early youth. Viswarup however was otherwise inclined; and filled with religious fervour, he left his home and turned a Sanyasi. The disconsolate mother had a yet severer trial awaiting her. It was not long after, that Jagannath Misra paid the debt of nature, and Nimai therefore was the sole surviving stay and consolation of the bereaved widow.

In his earlier days. Chaitanya had made the acquaintance of a girl named Lakshmi, daughter of Ballabhacharya, when she had come to the river-side to worship. The young student now thought of marriage, and his widowed mother celebrated his marriage with Lakshmi with feelings of mingled joy and sorrow.

As Chaitanya advanced in years, he began to gather round

him a large number of pupils, and his reputation as a scholar became great. The way in which philosophy, literature and religion have always been cultivated among the Hindus up to the time of the English conquest, and even since then, is well known. There were no regular academies, schools or colleges, as in Europe. The sages of ancient India, however, set themselves up as instructors, and gathered round them pupils varying in number according to their reputation for learning. Such pupils lived with their tutor in his house as members of the same family, looked on him as their father, and on his wife as their mother. Whatever might be their rank or status in society, they were all equal in his eyes, served him with equal fidelity during the period of their education, and vied with each other in obedience and respect towards him. The tutor received no fees, but the pupils looked to his cattle, milked his cows, begged food for his support, procured for him wood from the forest and water from the well, served him as his menial servants, and lived together in harmony and peace. When their education was completed, each pupil was expected to make a handsome present to his tutor, and this,—often a considerable sum of money,—was all that the *guru* received for his pains. Each pupil would then return to his own rank and status in life, a few of the more clever and advanced setting themselves up as new tutors and gathering pupils around them. The ancient lore of India has been handed down from generation to generation in this simple arcadian style, and vestiges of such institutions are still to be found in Nadiya and many other places in India. Thus under the Hindu, the Mahammadan, and even the English rule, these quiet thinkers and professors have from century to century preserved and propounded the ancient learning of India, and often started new questions in philosophy or law, despising all exotic wisdom and foreign languages, be it the Persian, the Arabic, or the English, and forgetting, and forgotten by, a world of unquiet and aspiring statesmen, politicians and men of the world.

Chaitanya, then, set himself up as a tutor, gathered pupils around him, and his fame as a man of deep learning increased day by day. His reputation spread throughout and beyond the limits of Nadiya. He baffled those who came to beat him in learned controversies, and satisfied others who came in all humility to have their doubts explained. After winning the admiration of all people in his native place, he left his country and travelled into Eastern Bengal. Thither too his fame had spread, and numbers of people flocked around him to have the benefit of his instructions. He reached the banks of the Padmavati and dwelt there for some months, instructing an ever increasing circle of friends. He then returned to his native place, but before he reached it his beloved wife had breathed her last.

Chaitanya continued to give instruction to his pupils at Nadiya; he was now called Nimai Pandit of Viswambhar Pandit. He assembled his pupils early in the morning and thaught them till about noon, after which he and his pupils went to the river-side together to bathe. Then they parted, and met again in the evening, and continued their literary labours till a later hours in the night.

The mother of Chaitanya became anxious to marry his son again, and the young Pandit was married to Vishnu Priya, the accomplished daughter of Sanatan whose learning had got for him the title of *Panditaraj*, or the prince of the learned. A pupil of Chaitanya, by name Buddhimanta, volunteered to pay the expenses of his tutor's marriage, and the ceremony was performed with great pomp. Soon after Chaitanya again left his native place and visited Gaya.

The visit to Gaya was the great turning point in the life of the reformer. Enthusiastic in his disposition, and attached to the faith of Krishna from his early youth, Chaitanya had, up to this time, lived and learned and taught much in the same way as other men did. But the sanctity of the place he visited, the instructions of Iswari Puri a devout Vaishnava, and the local religious associations of the place caused a thorough change in the character of the ardent young man. He had gone to Gaya a noted scholar and a religious man,—he returned an enthusiastic reformer.

Now, for the first time, were seen those violent outward manifestations of faith and feeling which characterized the ardent worshippers of Krishna in those times. Fired with unwonted zeal, they were now and then overtaken by paroxysms of faith, and wept and laughed and danced like mad men. Horripilation, violent perspiration and frequent fits of fainting morked these periods of religious ecstacy. The poor mother of Chaitanya trembled for her son, and marked with fear and concern the change in his demeanour, but it was beyond the power of domestic affection to make the reformer turn from the path he had chosen. It is not possible in the present age of reason to conceive the extent to which the mind can at times be subjected to the violent sway of religious feeling and fanaticism. Chaitanya was now a changed man; he fired in his followers and pupils an ardent faith in Krishna; he ignored all rites and ceremonies; he proclaimed from house tops that the salvation of man depended solely on faith in Krishna. The town of Nabadwip suddenly rang with the loud *Sankirtan* of Krishna.

Day after day, Chaitanya and his followers assembled and proclaimed and preached the faith of Krishna. They met in the house of Sribas, where Nityananda, Adyaita, Sridhar, and a number of other devout followers anointed Chaitanya with water, sandal powder and flowers. Their numbers daily increased; people of all classes were struck with the zeal and piety of the new sect; many joined it; and people of all castes and denominations were welcomed to seek salvation through faith in Krishna.

In the meanwhile the rise of this sect raised violent opposition in many quarters. Hindus looked with distrust and fear on a religion which ignored all rites and distinctions of caste, while the Muhammadan Kazi of the town ordered all Sankirtans to be forthwith stopped. Chaitanya, however. boldly met the Kazi, and the result of the interview, we are assured, was that the Kazi himself pronounced the holy name of Krishna and was saved. Many miracles are ascribed to Chaitanya about this period; but we pass them by.

Thus passed the first twenty-four years of the life of Chaitanya; and now he felt within him a powerful call to proclaim the light that was in him through the length and breadth of India. It was the small still voice which he could not resist, it was the call of duty which could not be silenced by the entreaties of friends or the tears of a mother. In vain did Sachi attempt with many tears to dissuade her only friend on earth from leaving her a forlorn helpless widow; in vain did even the devout followers of Chaitanya persuade him not to leave his native town. Chaitanya's heart was fixed and unmoved, and early in 1509, he became a Sanyasi and left his native town never to return again. During the remaining twenty-four years of his life he wandered as the apostle of Vaishnavism, and preached the faith of Krishna from the banks of the Cavery to the banks of the Jumna.

Chaitanya set out for Vrindavan on the banks of the Jumna, accompanied by Nityananda, Ratna and Mukunda, three of his followers. He crossed the Hugli, for Nabadwip was then on the east bank, and proclaimed the name of Krishna in every village through which he passed, to men, women and children. People were struck with his enthusiasm, and it is no wonder if many actually mistook the wild enthusiast for a deity. His follower Nityananda was one of those who would have liked to see his master always in his native town. It was not difficult to mislead Chaitanya from the right way to Vrindavan, and after three days' wanderings through several villages to the west of the Hugli, Nityananda brought back his master to the Hugli again. Chaitanya reproved his follower, but was obliged to cross the river and to rest for a few days in the town of Santipore. His follower Adyaita there received him with open arms and welcomed him to his house. News travelled to Nabadwip that the reformer had come back to Santipur, and all his friends and followers came to see him. Affecting indeed was the meeting of Chaitanya with his faithful followers whom he had left behind, but still more affecting was his meeting with his forlorn mother who came to Santipur to see his son once more. They insisted with many tears on his returning to Nabadwip, but Chaitanya had left his home as a Sanyasi and would not return. He consoled his mother however as best he could, assuring her that he would pass most of his time in Nilachala (Orissa), so that she would receive frequent news about him. To his followers he made the parting request that they should proclaim the name and religion of Krishna in their homes as he was going to proclaim it all over India. They parted once more, and Chaitanya set out on his travels.

Chaitanya now went southwards with Nityananda and others, passed through Jaipur, Cuttuck and Kamalpur, visited the shrines of Sakshi Gopal, Bhuvaneswar and Kapoteswar, and at last reached Jagannath. This last is a place dedicated to Krishna, and the deep veneration and ecstasy with which Chaitanya viewed this place may easily be conceived. There too he met Sarbabhauma, a learned and venerble man and a devout Vaishnava who received Chaitanya with open arms; and many and long were the religious controversies which they held together. From Jagannath, Chaitanya resolved to travel southwards. Nityananda and others offered to accompany him, but he wished to go alone, and was at last persuaded to take one Krishna Das, a simple-minded Brahman, as his sole companion. Southwards, then, went Chaitanya with Krishna Das, proclaiming the name of Krishna wherever he went. People flocked round him and were struck with his sanctity and enthusiasm, and numbers became converts. They returned to their villages, and told the wonderful tale and converted others. Thus, says the biographer of Chaitanya, the name of Krishna deluged the land as by an inundation.

At Jiar, Chaitanya rested a few days in the house of Ramananda Rai, a venerable and learned man, whom he instructed in the truths of his religion and soon fired with faith in Krishna. Thence he passed through numerous villages, everywhere making converts. Atheists, Philosophers of different schools, Buddhists, and Saivas, all yielded the palm to the new reformer, and many were the converts he made. At last he reached the banks of the Cavery and rested four months at Sriranga (Seringapatam). He visited the southern Mathura (Madura), and then Rameswar. Chaitanya also visited Kanya Kumari (Cape Comorin) and the Malaya or the Nilgiri Hills. Thence he travelled northwards, crossed the Tapti and the Nurbudda, and visited Dandakaranya, Pampa, Panchabati and other places noted in the Ramayana. Near the sources of the Godaveri he was joined by his old friend Ramananda Rai who had come here to meet him. They travelled back to Orissa, and at Jagannath, Chaitanya was met by most of his frends. His vows forbade him to return to his native place, but Krishna Das the companion of all his travels was sent to Nabadwip with the joyful tidings of his return. It was with great joy that his followers came and met him once more in Nilachala.

Chaitanya and his followers remained at Jagannath

during the Rath festival, and great were their rejoicings on the occasion. Prataparudra the king of Orissa expressed a desire to see the Vaishnava leader, but the Sanyasi's vow he had taken, forbade him to see a king. A sort of compromise was effected, the king's son visited the reformer, and Chaitanya blessed the father in the son, and they embraced his religion.

After a residence of a few months at Jagannath, Chaitanya resolved on visiting northern India. The king was distressed at this news, and Sarbabhauma, Ramananda and Nityananda, all tried to dissuade him from the undertaking. Their persuation however was fruitless, and at the close of the rainy season Chaitanya left Jagannath. He went northwards through Bhubaneswar, Cuttuck, Remuna and Panihati, and came once more to Santipur. Affecting indeed was his meeting with his mother who had come to Santipur from Nabadwip, and who embraced her son with tears of joy.

Chaitanya once more took leave of his friends, sent back his mother to Nabadwip, and left Santipur. Among his companions were the brothers Rup and Sanatan, ministers of the Muhammadan ruler of Behar.[3] They were of royal blood, and of high rank and much wealth, but despised all these things for their love of the reformer. Chaitanya's fame had now spread on all sides, and vast numbers of people gathered round him on his way towards Vrindavan. This was an inconvenience to a traveller, and Sanatan rightly advised him to part with all his companions if he wanted to proceed on his journey. The year however was far advanced, the rainy season had already commenced. Chaitanya therefore was compelled to remain a few months in Nilachala, to the great joy of king Prataprudra. At the close of the rains, he set out for Vrindavan with Balabhadra Bhattacharya as his sole companion.

To avoid notice Chaitanya left the beaten path, and went through a forest. His poetic biographer waxes eloquent,

[3] "They were two gifted men, originally Karṇāṭa Brāhmaṇs, settled for some generations in Bengal, who had adopted the Muhammadan name or title of Sāker Malik (Sanātana) and Dabir Khas (Rūpa) and were employed as high officials at the Muhammadan Court at Gauḍa." (S. K. De : *Early History of the Vaisnava Faith* etc. 73-74).—Ed.

and describes how in the presence of the great master the tiger embraced the deer and danced with joy, and how the name of Krishna, chanted by Chaitanya, made the flowers of the forest blossom and the birds chirp with glee. He passed through Benares and Allahabad, proclaiming the name of Krishna and making numerous converts as he went along. Great indeed was his ecstacy when he at last gazed on the Jumna and visited Mathura and Vrindavan. His whole life had been spent in proclaiming the name of Krishna, and his fervour and his ardent love reached their climax when he witnessed the scenes of Krishna's boyhood and early youth. His paroxysms of feeling came over him thick and frequent, and his life was endangered by the repeated fits of fainting that he underwent. From these scenes Chaitanya returned to Allahabad by the river. Here he was met by the brothers Rup and Ballabh, who had sacrificed wealth, rank and royal favour, and become devout Vaishnavas. Their eldest brother Sanatan had in the meantime got into a scrape. He too had resigned his service, but the king would not let him go so easily. Incensed at the conduct of Rup and Ballabh, the king ordered Sanatan to be confined. Escaping after many difficulties, Sanatan at last joined Chaitanya at Benares. Both Rup and Sanatan were learned men and authors of note, as we shall see in a future chapter, and long and numerous were the religious dialogues between Chaitanya and Sanatan at Benares. Sanatan was then sent to join his brothers at Vrindavan to preach the name of Krishna, and Chaitanya once more returned to his loving friends at Nilachala.

The remaining years of his life were passed by Chaitanya in Nilachala in meditations and in preaching the name of Krishna. His devoted followers occasionally came to visit him, the brothers Rup, Sanatan and Ballabh came from Vrindavan and were received by Chaitanya with joy, but they were again sent back to Vrindavan. Raghunath Das was also sent to Vrindavan. Nityananda and others remained with Chaitanya in Nilachala.

A curious story is told of the death of Chaitanya. One evening, as he was wandering on the sea-beach with his friends, he was suddenly struck at the sight of the bright moon-beams glittering on the blue waves of the sea. In one of those paroxysms which were so frequent with him, he mistook the sea for the blue waves of the Jumma. He ran into the sea in ecstacy, and soon after became insensible. His friends missed him and searched for him every where, and soon after, a fisherman brought to his disconsolate followers the body of their beloved master which he had fished up from the sea. Chaitanya died in 1533 at the early age of 48.

Such was the life of the great apostle of Hindu monotheism in Bengal. Chaitanya did not found a new religion. His religion is only a reformed phase of the Hindu religion. It recognizes Krishna as the Supreme Deity, ignores the caste system, and even admits Muhammadans as proselytes. In the present day, however, all lay Vaishnavas have adopted Hinduism and recognize the caste system, and it is only among the mendicant Vaishnavas that the religion of Chaitanya is found to prevail in its integrity. In this respect Vaishnavism resembles Buddhism which has its monks and its lay disciples; and indeed scholars are aware that Vaishnavism itself is a modern survival of Buddhism under a Hindu guise. Buddhism in an idolatrous form prevailed during many centuries after the Christian era in Orissa, and the worship of Buddha, recognized by Hindus as one of the incarnations of Vishnu, now survives in a Hindu guise in the worship of Jagannath.

CHAPTER VII

The Followers of Chaitanya (Sixteenth Century)

We have in the preceding chapter given a sketch of the life and work of Chaitanya. In the present chapter we shall very briefly review the work of some of the companions of the reformer,—the Apostles of Vaishnavism in Bengal.[1]

Among the followers of Chaitanya, Advaita and Nityananda stand foremost. Indeed, the Vaishnavas of Bengal regard them as partial incarnations of Vishnu, as part and parcel of the spirit which had its full manifestation in Chaitanya.

In the preceding chapter we have had frequent occasions to notice the acts of these leaders, nor is there much to add. Advaita was a wealthy and respected inhabitant of Santipur, and is said to have prophesied the birth of Chaitanya, and sent his wife to Nabadwip when the great reformer was born. After Chaitanya had left his home as a Sanyasi, never to return, the house of Advaita at Santipur was more than once the meeting place where the Vaishnavas of Bengal flocked to see their master, returned from his travels. All through his life, Advaita, though himself a wealthy man, held the poor wandering reformer in deep veneration. The descendants of Advaita still live in Santipur, and are held by all Vaishnavas in the highest regard.

Nityananda was perhaps the most esteemed companion of Chaitanya. He was a wealthy inhabitant of Nabadwip, and is said to have been by no means indifferent to the good things of this life. Yet Chaitanya held him in high respect and bestowed on him the title of *Probhu*. His descendents are yet living. The Goswamis of Khardaha are descended from him by the male line, and those of Balagor by the female line. Chaitanya. Advaita and Nityananda are spoken of by the

[1] For much of the information contained in this chapter we are indebted to Ram Das Sen's paper on the works of the Vaishnava Leaders of Bengal.

N.B. :—For up-to-date information the reader may refer to S. K. De : *Early History of Vaisnava Faith etc.*, Revised edition, Cal.—Ed.

Vaishnavas of Bengal as the three Prabhus. They were all Brahmans by birth, and none of them seems to have written any books either in Sanscrit or in Bengali.

Next to these came the six great writers who are known as the Vaishnavacharyas of Bengal. They are Rup Goswami, Sanatan Goswami, Jiva Goswami, Gopal Bhatta, and Raghunath Das. It is much to be regretted that they have all written in Sanskrit,—the highest efforts of their genius appear feeble and commonplace because they are misdirected. High indeed, in the rolls of the early Bengali authors, had the names of Rup and Sanatan stood, if they had written in their native tongue. As it is, their names are generally known only among Vaishnavas, and the proud position which they might have occupied is ceded to Mukunda Ram and other writers who composed in the language of the people. It is a lesson which has a special application in the present day.

We have already noticed the prominent facts in the lives of the brothers Rup and Sanatan in the preceding chapter. They were of royal blood, being descended from a prince of the Carnatic, and held high positions under the Muhammadan ruler of Behar. Fanatics and enthusiasts have already succeeded in gathering round them a number of ignorant people, but the reformer of the sixteenth century must have indeed had a strange power to induce men of wealth and influence to descend from their high position in society, to be his humble followers. Rup and Sanatan gave up their posts, sacrificed wealth, rank and royal favour, disregarded royal wrath, and braved persecution, in order to become humble Vaishnavas.

Rup Goswami has written several books. *Ujjvala Nilamani* is a book on Sanscrit rhetoric in prose and verse. Under the plea of describing the life and acts of Krishna, the writer discourses on love, piety and devotion. *Hansa Duta* describes the distress of Radha and the milk-maids of Gokula in the absence of Krishna. They at last send a goose as a messenger to Krishna, and hence the name of the book. *Uddhava Sandesa* describes the agony of Krishna in the absence of Radha, and the lover at last sends Uddhava as a messenger to the beloved, hence the name of the book. *Srirupa Chintamani* describes the beauty of Krishna, and *Mathura*

Mahatmya, as the name implies, describes the glory of Mathura. Many other poems also were written by this voluminous versifier.

Sanatan Goswami has written very much less than his brother. His *Gitavali* describes the Doljatra, Rasa, and other festivities held in honor of Krishna.

Jiva Goswami was the son of Ballabh, the brother of Rup and Sanatan. His great work is *Shat Sandarbha* which, as its name signifies, is divided into six parts, and describes religious and devotional feelings.

Gopal Bhatta was the son of Benkata Bhatta of the village Bhattamari. During his travels Chaitanya stopped for a period of four months in his house, and the religious fervour and instructions of the reformer left an impression on the mind of the young Bhatta. Soon after the departure of Chaitanya, Gopal left home and family and turned a wanderer like his master. He stopped for a time at Benares with a learned teacher, and turning a regular Sanyasi went to Vrindavan. where he joined Rup, Sanatan and other Vaishnava luminaries. He wrote several works, of which *Haribhakti-vilasa* is the best known. It treats of the duties of Vaishnavas.

Raghunath Das was a Kayastha by birth, and the son of a wealthy man. The *Bhaktamala* states that he left property worth nine lacs and a young wife of exceeding beauty and loveliness for his love of Chaitanya. He met the reformer at Jagannath, and Chaitanya held him in great esteem and love. Afterwards he went to Vrindavan and lived with the celebrated Vaishnavas of that place. Though a Kayastha by birth, he received from Chaitanya the title of Acharya, and lived with the five other Acharyas. These last were all Brahmans by birth, but neither Chaitanya nor his followers recognized caste inequalities. His *Vilapakusumanjali Stotra* is the prayer of a devout Vaishnava perplexed with the troubles of this world, and his *Manosiksha* treats of the training of the mind to the love of Krishna.

Krishna Das. Vrindavan Das and Lochan Das, the biographers of Chaitanya, though not strictly speaking his companions, may come in for a notice here. They have written in Bengali, and their works are very popular with Vaishnavas.

Vrindavan Das was the son of Narayani who from her

girlhood was devotedly attached to the faith of Chaitanya. Pandit Ramgati has erroneously supposed her to be the daughter of Srivas a follower of Chaitanya. The author himself informs us that his mother was the daughter of a brother of Srivas.[2] And it was in the house of Srivas that the little girl, then four years old, first saw the reformer, and ever after loved him and his religion. It would appear therefore, that Vrindavan Das wrote his book about the middle of the 16th century, and after the death of Chaitanya.

We confess we cannot discover much beauty or poetic excellence in his book *Chaitanya Bhagavat*, and if it is a popular book with Vaishnavas we can only ascribe the fact to its being the first book describing the life and acts of Chaitanya. Krishna Das is lavish in his praise of Vrindavan's work, and indeed compares Vrindavan to the great Vyasa of ancient India. But we confess we turn with a sort of relief from Vrindavan's affected style and dreary Sanscrit quotations to the simpler narrative of Krishna Das himself.

Krishna Das was born at Jhamatpur near Katwa in the district of Burdwan, and was a Vaidya by caste. He was a devout Vaishnava and travelled to Vrindavan, in which place he probably composed his *Chaitanya Charitamrita*. The date of the book is not known. Very probably it was written some twenty years after Vrindavan Das had written his book. It is, we think, in every respect superior to the work of Vrindavan Das; the style is simple, and the writer apparently writes with feeling. The description of the rejoicings in Nabadwip at the birth of Chaitanya, the account of Sachi's parting with her beloved son, and the description of the Rathajatra ceremony at Jagannath, are all instinct with feeling.

The third biography of Chaitanya is *Chaitanya Mangal* of Lochan Das. It is not considered a book of high authority by the Vaishnavas.

Other voluminous Vaishnava works like Narahari's *Bhaktiratnakar* and Madhava's *Bhagavatsara*, well-known works in their days, are now well nigh forgotten. Madhava is said to have also written a work on *Chandi* which has been replaced by the more meritorious work composed by Mukundaram.

[2] Vide pp. 123 of *Chaitanya Bhāgavat*.

CHAPTER VIII

RAGHUNATH AND HIS SCHOOL OF LOGIC (SIXTEENTH CENTURY)

HISTORY repeats itself. The human mind often moves forward in the same direction, and by the same path, when inspired with fresh vigour and fresh light. There can be little in common between the age of rationalism and reform in ancient India, — the sixth century before Christ, and the age of renaissance in modern India, — the sixteenth century after Christ. The Hindu nation was free and the Hindu mind was untrammelled in the ancient age; the nation was subject to a foreign rule and its energies and thoughts were cribbed and confined in the modern age. But nevertheless it is impossible not to recognize in the renaissance of the sixteenth century after Christ a pale reflection of the movement which was witnessed in the sixth century before Christ.

Buddhism had almost died out in Bengal, but it was Buddhist monastic institutions and Buddhist principles of human equality and brotherhood which were renovated in a Hindu guise in modern Vaishnavism. And Chaitanya therefore is the modern counterpart of Gautama Buddha. Ancient Hindu philosophy and logic were scarcely known in Bengal before the sixteenth century; it was in that *siecle* that the philosophical school of Nabadwip was started, and Raghunath is the modern counterpart of Kapila. And lastly, Hindu orthodoxy was alarmed at the spread of heterodox and philosophical speculations in ancient India as in modern Bengal, sacred laws and rules of orthodox rites were carefully compiled and insisted upon, and Raghunandan of modern Bengal is the counterpart of Vasishtha and Gautama and other ancient compilers of sacred laws. We are afraid to proceed further with this parallel; it would be misleading to suggest a very close resemblance between India in the sixth century, B. C. and India in the sixteenth century A. D. All that we wish to indicate is that the Hindu mind in modern age has, under the influence of new light and progress, travelled once more in the same direction, though with feeble effort, as it did in the days of its ancient vigour.

Mithila or North Behar was one of the most advanced kingdoms in India from the time of Janaka in the epic age, and took a prominent part in the progress of philosophy and thought which marked the seventh and sixth centuries before Christ. It is possible that Gautama the founder of logic flourished in Behar; it is certain that logical studies were kept up in the schools of Mithila by an uninterrupted succession of scholars and teachers. Pakshadhara Misra was the last of these eminent scholars, and had his crowded *tol* of logic in Mithila in the fifteenth century; and Vasudeb of Nabadwip was one of the scholars who learnt logic in his school.

Vasudeb returned to Nabadwip with the title of Sarbabhaoma. and set himself up as a teacher, and the three great men whose deeds have shed a bright light on the sixteenth century, — Chaitanya, Raghunath and Raghunandan, — all received their insttruction in their early days from this prince of teachers.

Raghunath was a poor orphan and was blind of one eye from his birth. In school he often puzzled the venerable Vasudeb by his questions, and his eager and inquisitive mind was not satisfied with the traditional solutions of difficult problems. It is said that young Chaitanya and young Raghunath were intimate friends, and that the doubts and anxious enquiries of Raghunath were often solved for him by the future reformer with his clear intellect and his strong natural good sense. Raghunath thanked his friend for such assistance, and hoped to pursue philosophical studies with him through life. But their paths lay in different directions; Chaitanya went in for religious reform, and Raghunath, at the early age of twenty, left his home and repaired to Mithila to complete his study of logic in that renowned "university-town."

Old Pakshadhara Misra was still alive, and welcomed his pupil's pupil to his school. In a short time however he perceived that the mind of the young man was cast in a different mould from that of ordinary students, and that traditional learning did not satisfy him. Many were the enquiries with which the young student puzzled his venerable teacher, and the fame of Raghunath spread far and wide.

It was necessary for a student on the completion of his education to signalize himself in a trial, and to win his title. Young Raghunath fearlessly entered into a discussion with his teacher, and did not hesitate to demolish his arguments. But it was not possible for the venerable Professor of logic to confess a defeat in the very place where generations of students had looked up to him as infallible. With a pardonable weakness, Pakshadhara concealed his defeat in a cloud of sophistry, and humiliated his ardent opponent with bitter taunts and ridicule. Young Raghunath left the school humiliated, and to all appearance beaten in the discussion.

A story is then told for the accuracy of which it is impossible to vouch, but which is worth repeating. Smarting under disgrace and undeserved humiliation, the young student is said to have sought the house of his teacher by night, on vengeful thoughts intent. The object of his ambition was lost, and his prospect in life was ruined; for it would be impossible to convince the Hindu world that the great Pakshadhara was wrong and the unknown young student was right. His apparent defeat and humiliation had ruined his prospects; he could win no title now and could open no school, no students would gather round him and no one would credit his acquirements and learning. A blow had been struck. such as only the heavy hand of a man, great in rank and reputation, can strike on an unknown but aspiring youth. The blow had fallen with fatal effect and it was impossible to recover from it; and the career for which young Raghunath had laboured for years, and which was the dream of his ambition, was lost for ever. Raghunath was a ruined man, and Raghunath stole into his teacher's house,—a desperate man.

The light of the full-moon fell on Pakshadhara's house as the old professor and his wife sat on the roof. The gentle housewife was trying to please her husband, but something troubled him and preyed on him. He seldom replied to her and scarcely heard what she said. To all appearance he had demolished young Raghunath in the discussion held that day, but the good old teacher could not forgive himself the art he had practised, and he felt within himself that for once in his life he had been fairly beaten, though none knew it.

Pakshadhara woke from his reveries when his gentle wife

spoke of the moon-beams and asked,—"Is there anything in this world, lord, which is clearer and brighter than the light of the autumn moon?" "Yes, lady," replied involuntarily the hoary professor, "there is a young student who has come to my school from Nabadwip;—his intellect is brighter and clearer than the light of the autumn moon."

Raghunath heard this conversation, his angry thoughts were dispelled, he rushed forward and fell at his beloved professor's feet. Pakshadhara raised him and embraced him, and the next day he confessed and proclaimed before all that Raghunath had really beaten him in the discussion of the preceding day. The triumph of Raghunath was complete, and he returned to Nabadwip and founded the school of logic in that place which has continued to be the most renowned school of logic in India during these three centuries.

The story narrated above probably only gives a concrete shape to the fact that, since the sixteenth century, the school of logic at Mithila has declined, and the school of logic at Nabadwip has prospered. An uninterrupted line of renowned logicians have flourished in that town from the time of Raghunath to the present day.[1]

Raghunath was still a poor man, but learning has always been honoured in this country by high and low alike, and it is said that a substantial cowherd of the name of Hari Ghosh helped the young professor to build his *tol*. Students from all parts of India came to the scholar who had beaten Pakshadhara in logic, and Raghunath lived to be a great and a famous man.

His great work in logic is *Chintamani Didhiti*. Any attempt to explain the contents of this book would be beyond the scope of the present volume.

[1] I paid a visit to a *tol* of logic in Nabadwip in 1876, and met students there from all parts of India. On my asking them the reason of their coming to Bengal for education, they told me that while the Vedas were taught at Benares, and other branches of learning in other places, Logic was nowhere taught as thoroughly as at Nabadwip.

CHAPTER IX

RAGHUNANDAN AND HIS INSTITUTES (SIXTEENTH CENTURY)

WE have remarked in the preceding chapter that Mithila or North Behar was one of the most cultured kingdoms in ancient India. Among all the nations of the Epic Age, the Videhas of Mithila were considered the most cultured. And when the nations of the Epic Age declined in power, the Magadhas of South Behar took the lead, and were for centuries the most powerful and the most enlightened nation in India. There can be little doubt that Bengal was first colonized by Aryans from Behar, *i.e.,* from the sister kingdoms of Mithila and Magadha, and that for two thousand years Bengal received culture and knowledge from her western sisters. And when the light of modern literature and philosophy and religious reform dawned on Bengal in the fourteenth, fifteenth and sixteenth centuries, we still mark that the light proceeded from the west. Chandidas's poetry was inspired by Bidyapati and other poets of Mithila; Chaitanya's reform was a survival and a revival of the monastic Buddhism of Magadha; Raghunath's school of logic was an offshoot of the schools of Mithila; and lastly Raghunandan's compilation of sacred laws was in imitation of such compilations made in Mithila.

Since the sixteenth century, however, Bengal has taken the lead. Chandidas has been followed by a host of poets and writers in Bengal, down to the present century, whose equals Behar has not produced. Vaishnavism still flourishes in Bengal, and has been succeeded by the more enlightened Brahmoism, based on the same principles of human equality and brotherhood, while Magadha has witnessed no religious reforms in modern times. And lastly the philosophical school of Raghunath, founded in Nabadwip, is at the present day the most renowned school of Hindu logic in India, while philosophy and logic have declined in Mithila.

The compilation of sacred laws for the regulation of

the conduct of Aryan Hindus began in India before the time of Buddha; and in those days each Sutra-Charana or distinct Sutra school had its separate body of laws for the use of the followers of that particular school. The Charanyavyuha names five distinct Charanas or schools of the Rig Veda, twenty-seven of the Black Yajur Veda, fifteen of the White Yajur Veda, twelve of the Sama Veda, and nine of the Atharva Veda.

The spread of Buddhism somewhat dislocated the old arrangements, and the distinctions between the separate Sutra schools were lost. The Institutes of Manu, which in their existing form belong approximately to the time of Christ, do not connect themselves with any particular Sutra school, but profess to be the rules for all Aryan Hindus. In other respects, however, Manu's institutes are still archaic; they recognize Vedic gods and Vedic sacrifices, and ignore the modern Hindu Trinity, and condemn the worship of images.

In later times, after the decline of the old Hindu races of Northern India, and even after the conquest of India by the Muhammadans, bodies of sacred law still continued to be compiled or recast. And these modern compilations, like those of Vyasa and Parasara, inculcate modern Hinduism and modern usages, and the worship of images.

The entire body of sacred laws, *viz.*, the Sutras, Manu's Institutes, and the later law books, are spoken of together as *Smriti;* and the study of *Smriti* is still a very important portion of orthodox training all over India. It may well be imagined that the study of Smriti was not neglected in Mithila, and spread from Mithila to Bengal.

In the ninth century after Christ, Medhatithi flourished in Mithila, and wrote the first great and authoritative commentary on Manu's institutes. Bengal followed the lead, and soon distanced her western sister. Kullukabhattta was the son of Dibakarabhatta, and was born near Gaur in the fourteenth century. His commentary on Manu's Institues has almost replaced all others, and has been pronounced by so great an autthority as Sir William Jones to be the most clear, the most concise, and the most perspicuous commentary that has ever been written.

In the eleventh century after Christ, Vijnanesvara of

Western India compiled the law of succession, called the Mitakshara, which prevails in Behar and in the west. The law of succession in Bengal is somewhat different; and in the fourteenth century, Jimutavahana of Bengal compiled the Dayabhaga, which has since been considered the authoritative work on Hindu succession in Bengal. Colebrooke has translated both Mitakshara and Dayabhaga into English.

But it was left to Raghunandan to compile a complete code of rules for religious rites and observances, as they obtain in Bengal in the modern age. Raghunandan was also of Nabadwip, and was by about twenty years junior to Chaitanya and Raghunath; and he is said to have also received his early training from the venerable Vasudeb Sarbabhauma. No other school master in the world has perhaps turned out such three brilliant and great men as Chaitanya, Raghunath and Raghunandan!

While Chaitanya devoted himself to religious reform, while Raghunath spent his life in philosophical and logical studies, Raghunandan made his mark by an authoritative and exhaustive compilation of the rules of orthodox rites and observances for the people of Bengal. He divided this great work into twenty-eight chapters, each devoted to a separate subject,[1] and he based his rules on a profusion of quotations from the highest authorities. He laboured for twenty-five years over this great work, and it remains a monument, not only of his industry and learning, but also of his comprehensive genius.

It is needless to state that Raghunandan's Institutes, though still considered the authoritative work in the matter of rites and observances in Bengal, is losing its importance with the progress of the times. An orthodox work which insists with the utmost rigour on distinctions between Brah-

1. He himself specifies twenty-eight subjects thus :—
malimluce dāyabhāge saṁskāre śuddhi-nirṇaye|
prāyaścitte vivāhe ca tithau janmāṣṭamīvrate||
durgotsave vyavahṛtāvekādaśyādi-nirṇaye|
taḍāga-bhavanotsarge vṛṣotsarge-traye vrate||
pratiṣṭhāyām parīkṣāyām jyotiṣe vāstu-yajñake|
dīkṣāyām āhnike kṛtye kṣetre śrī-puruṣottame||
sāma-śrāddhe yajuḥ-śrāddhe śūdrakṛtya-vicāraṇe|
ityaṣṭāriṁśati-sthāne tattvam vakṣyāmi yatnataḥ||

mans and non-Brahmans (miscalled Sudras) must lose its weight in a age when the non-Brahmans also claim to be true born Aryan Hindus, entitled to the learning and the privileges of Aryan Hindus. A work which multiplies and insists on puerile rites and hurtful restrictions must become obsolete, when the rites are ignred and the restrictions are disregarded, in pursuit of progress and national well-being. A work which lays down the duties of Hindu widows with cruel severity, and recommends the burning of widows on the pyre, must fall into disrepute when widow-marriage has been legalized, and the burning of widows has been stamped out as an offence and a crime against humanity. A more advanced and healthier compilation of rules for the social and religious use of modern Hindus, based on their ancient scriptures, has become a desideratum.

These remarks should not be considered as a reflection against Raghunandan ; it is no fault of that great compiler that the times have changed, and that the rules compiled by him are no longer observed. The scholar and the student can respect the laws of Manu or of Justinian, although those laws have become obsolete among modern Hindus and modern Romans.

The school of *Smriti* started by Raghunandon still continues in Nabadwip. Eminent teachers have handed down the traditional learning from generation to generation, and students still attend the *Smriti tols* of that classic town, the Oxford of Bengal.

Besides *Nyaya*, and *Smriti* other branches of Sanscrit learning have also been studied in Bengal. In *Vyakarana* or grammar, Bopadeva of Bengal[2] is the greatest writer that modern India has produced. And Krishnananda of Nabadwip, who was a contemporary of Chaitanya, was a great compiler of *Tantra* literature a literature which flourishes in Bengal only among all the provinces of India. We do not believe however that the other provinces lose much by the absence of this class of literature, as it only reproduces Buddhist

[2] There is no positive evidence of this author having been a Bengali. —Ed.

superstitious rites and practices in a Hindu guise, with much that is dark, cruel and reprehensible. Similar Tantra works and Tantra practices are known in Thibet and other Buddhist countries to this day.

CHAPTER X.

MUKUNDA RAM AND HIS CHANDI
(SEVENTEENTH CENTURY)

THE brilliant sixteenth century, which witnessed the rise of Chaitanya, Raghunath and Raghunandan in Bengal, also witnessed the conquest of that country by the great Akbar, with the help of his Hindu generals Todar Malla and Man Sinha. These events influenced the national mind, and the first original poem in Bengali, apart from songs and translations, was composed in the seventeenth century. Mukunda Ram Chakrabarti has fortunately left us some account of himself and his times. He was born in the village of Daminya, near Salimabad, in the District of Burdwan. He was the son of Hriday Misra, and the grandson of Jagannath Misra, and he had an elder brother of the name of Kabi Chandra. He tells us that when Man Sinha became the ruler of Bengal, the oppression of a sub-ordinate Muhammadan officer drove him from his home, and that after long wanderings he found a kind protector in Bankura Deb, a Zemindar in the District of Midnapur. The seat of the Zemindar was in the village of Anra, and he engaged the learned guest as a tutor to his son, Raghunath, who subsequently succeeded his father in the estate, and finds frequent mention in the poet's work.

It is so seldom that a poet leaves us an account of himself and his times, that we cannot resist the temptation of quoting the whole of the account left by Mukunda Ram in a note.[1] We give the substance of it in English.

The ancestors of Mukunda Ram to the sixth or seventh generation lived in the petty village of Daminya, engaged in agricultural pursuits. It appears that when Man Sinha became the ruler of Bengal, Muhammad Sharif, an oppressive man, was invested with power and influence, and as a consequence the people were grievously oppressed. Brahmans and Vaishnavas, traders and agriculturists, were subjected to equal

[1] For considerations of space, we have omitted the quotation.—Ed.

tyranny; fallow lands were entered as arable; 15 kathas of lond were reckoned as a bigha by a various system of measurement. Every Rupee was short by 2½ annas. The agriculturists began to sell off their cattle and grain, of which there was a glut in the market, so that things of the value of a rupee sold for 10 annas. Gopinath Nandi, the Talukdar under whom the poet held his lands, and who is described as a pious man, got into a scrape and was imprisoned.

After consultation with the wise Srimanta Khan of Chandibati, our poet left the home of his fathers in bitter grief to seek shelter elsewhere. He reached Bhetna, where Jadu Kundu, as the poet gratefully records, gave him food and shelter for three days. Honest Jadu Kundu! Little did he dream when, in compliance with one of the most amiable customs of the country, he gave shelter to a poor houseless stranger, that for his good service, for which he sought no return, his name would live in immortal verse. The poet then went down the Gharai and crossed the Darakeswar, and reached Pandurpur, where Gangadas did him some service. At last Mukunda Ram crossed the Damodar and reached Kuchutya in much distress, the children crying for food. Oppressed with hunger, the poet fell asleep near a tank, and saw the goddess Chandi in a vision, and she bade him sing her glory. Soon after, the poet found shelter in the village of Anra in the district of Midnapur, where he accosted the zemindar Bankura Deb in verse for which he was rewarded with five *aris* of dhan. The zemindar received the talented stranger with open arms, and engaged him as a tutor to his son, Raghunath. In those days zemindars delighted in gathering learned and talented men round them, and as there was no reading public, this was the only sort of encouragement that learning received.

Mukunda Ram, who obtained the title of Kabi Kankan, had two sons, Sivaram and Mahesh, and two daughters Chitrarekha and Jashoda. The descendants of the poet still live, not in Daminya, but in the neighbouring village of Bainan. The descendants of Raghunath, the pupil and protector of the poet, live in Senapat a village about four miles from Anra; their estates have all been taken over by the Raja of Burdwan.

Mukunda Ram has left us two poems. The first is the tale of Kalaketu, a hunter, and his wife Fullara; and the other one is the celebrated story of Srimanta Sadagar. We will briefly narrate the plot of each poem.

The book begins, as usual, with prayers to several gods and goddesses, and with an account of Chandi, her previous existence as the daughter of Daksha, the destruction of his celebrated sacrifice by Siva, Chandi's second birth as the daughter of the Himalayas, the destruction of Kama, the grief and religious penances of Chandi, and her final union with Siva.[3] Then follows the story of Kalaketu.

Kalaketu the hero of the poem is a hunter of low birth, and proves to be the strongest among the strong. He frequents the wood every day with his bow and arrows, and kills wild beasts, often fighting numbers of them single-handed. His fame as a brave young hunter increases day by day, and in course of time he is married to Fullara. The married life of Kalaketu and Fullara has been well depicted by the poet, and the strongest impression that one receives from a perusal of the poem is its intense reality. The hunter, strong and robust, but somewhat rude in his habits, frequents the forests and lives on the proceeds of his spoil. And the poor but faithful Fullara takes the meat to the market, cooks food for her husband, and administers to his wants like a careful housewife that she is.

But Chandi will not allow her favourite Kalaketu to pine in poverty. She appears in his hut during his absence as a woman of superb beauty, and gives Fullara to understand that she is desirous of sharing with her the affections of Kalaketu. Poor, simple-minded Fullara! She is in a great fright at seeing a rival of such beauty, and with ill-concealed jealousy she advises her to return to her husband, and never to leave the paths of virtue. A long conversation ensues, and

[3] For want of space we are unable to make any extracts, but the reader will find many passages in this part of the work full of the choicest humour. We would refer him to the disputes between Hara and Parvati, as well as to the regrets of women at their own evil fate, when they see the handsome face and form of the bridegroom, Siva. Most of our readers know the celebrated passages of Bharat Chandra on similar subjects, but most of them do not know that these passages of Bharat Chandra are only imitations from the original of Mukunda Ram.

the whole is one of the most interesting passages in the work. The fair intruder however is immovable, and we almost think we see the smile of ridicule which curls her sweet lips as the listens to her rival. Fullara then discourses on her own sorrows, and tries to dissuade the fair visitant from sharing them, and the eloquence with which she dwells on her poverty and troubles all the twelve months in the year, would almost affect any listener. But the disguised goddess says, truly enough, that she has wealth of her own with which she will make Kalaketu happy. Throughout the passage the replies of the goddess have a double meaning. Most of our Bengali readers are familiar with the account in Bharat Chandra's poetry, which Chandi gives of herself to Isvar the ferryman when he takes her across the river. The goddess, while virtually giving a true account of herself, makes the ferryman believe that she is a poor woman who has left her husband's home in grief. But most of our readers are *not* aware that the passage is only a copy of a similar passage in Mukunda Ram's poetry, and in some places it is a copy word for word.[3] We

[3] We give a few extracts here from the remarkable conversation between Fullara and Chandi, but prudently refrain from venturing to translate them into English.

sakhi gṛhe khud ser kariyā udhār|
sambhrame phullarā āilā kūḍiyā duyār||

* * * *

phullarāre abhayā karen upahās||
ilavṛte ghar mor jātite brāhmaṇī |

* * * *

vandya vamśe sthiti more rāperā ghoṣāl
sāt satā gṛhe vās viṣam jañjāl||
tumi go phullarā yadi deo anumati|
ei sthāne katak din kariye rasati ||

* * * *

Fullara says :

erūp yauvane chāḍiyā bhavane
kene āilā paravās|
kaha go sundarī kene ekeśvarī
bhramite nāhi tarās||

* * * *

The goddess in disguise says :—

* * * *

ki kava duḥkher kathā gaṅgā nāme mor satā
svāmi yāre dharaye mastake |

should add that here, as elsewhere, the extracts we have given from Mukunda Ram are from the scholarly edition of his works compiled from old manuscripts.

Poor Fullara, when she finds all her entreaties and tears are of no avail, leaves the hut and goes to meet her husband in the agony of her heart. She returns with Kalaketu who is equally struck at the remarkable beauty of the fair visitant, but politely rebukes her for coming along into his house. Chandi makes no reply, on which Kalaketu, with his accustmed boorrishness, wants to send her out somewhat unceremoniously, and even takes to his bow and arrows. But lo! his strength fails him, and he stands like a pictured warrior, unable to shoot. Chandi then discovers herself, and to make a long story short, points out the spot where gold and treasures are buried, and Kalaketu becomes a rich man. By order of Chandi he hews down a forest, and founds a new town dedicated to the goddess.

In his account of the founding of the new town the poet gives us a graphic picture of the manners of the times in which the work was written. The way in which raiyats were induced to settle in a new village, the rights and immunities promised to them, the loan of cattle and grain and money given them, the different customs of the people of different

varañca garal khāy ámā pāne nāhi cāy
bhavan tyajinu sei śoke||

* * * *

ugra āmār pati hailām avalā jāti
pāñc mukhe gāli pāḍe kope|
eke satiner jvālā kata sahe avalā
lāje jalāñjali dinu tāpe||

* * * *

śatek rājār dhan añge mor ābharaṇ
bhuvan kinite pāri dhane|
sampad vistar diva keval bhakati niva
śri kavikañkaṇ ras bhaṇe||

* * * *

Fullara says :—

tore āmi bali bhāla svāmir vasati cala
pariṇāme pāve vaḍa dukh|

* * * *

svāmīi param dhan svāmi vine anya jan
keha nahe sukh-mokṣa dātā||

faiths and castes,—Muhammadans, Brahumans, Vaidyas, Kayasthas, Goalas, Telis, Kamars, Kumars, &c., all this has been depicted with a fidelity and photographic minuteness unequalled in the whole range of Bengali literatture.

Among the men who come to dwell in the new town, Gujrat, is one Bharu Datta an astute Kayastha and an impudent impostor. The poet has displayed a remarkable power in delineating this character. His vanity is unbounded, and the coolest impudence supplies the place of real worth. We subjoin a passage in which Bharu Datta at his first meeting with Kalaketu gives a boastful account of himself. There is a vein of the richest humour pervading the passage.[4]

The late hunter is no good judge of character; he takes Bharu Datta at his word, and honours him and entrusts him with power. Such men when invested with power invariably turn oppressive, and Bharu Datta is no exception to the rule. The people loudly murmur, and Kalaketu finds out his mistake and turns Bharu out of his office. With his usual effrontery and cunning, Bharu goes over to the King Kalinga, arouses his jealousy at the sudden greatness of Kalaketu, and brings about a war between the two kings. Kalaketu is beaten and confined, but Chandi will not desert her follower. She appears in a vision to the King of Kalinga; and the next morning Kalaketu is released and sent to his own country, and Bharu Datta is disgraced.

The story of Srimanta Sadagar, which forms the subject of the second poem of Mukunda Ram, is so well known to most of our readers that a brief account of it will suffice. Dhanapati, a *Gandha Banik* by caste and trader by profession, exhibits his pigeons to the king one day, and it so happens that one of the pigeons flies off and drops where Knullana a

[4] *bheṭ layā kāṁchalā paścāte bhāṅḍur sala*
āgu bhāṅḍudatter payān |
* * * *
praṇām kariyā vire bhāṁḍu nivedan kare
* * * *
yatek kāyastha dekha bhāṁḍur paścāte lekha
kule śile vicāre mahattve||
* * * *
āmi pātra tumi rāja ihā jāni kara pūjā
avaśeṣe bhāṁḍure jānive||

girl of twelve is playing. Dhanapati goes to her and demands her pigeon, and is at the same time pleased with the amiable face and demeanour of the young girl. His wife is a cousin of Khullana, and as merry repartees are allowed between such relatives, Khullana replies to him merrily and wittily. Proposals follow, and Khullana's father consents to the match. But his wife Rambhabati naturally hesitates to give her only girl to a man who has already a wife, and administers a sound curtain lecture to her mate, spiced with such mild epithets as *paḍe śune haile paśu,* with which many a careful house-wife in modern as well as in ancient times has expressed her kind regards for her husband. The bridegroom Dhanapati too, has the benefit of a similar lecture from his wife Lahana, cousin of Khullana, for wishing to marry again at this mature age; but a kind word turneth away wrath, and Dhanapati knows the truth of the saying. He accosts Labana in the politest of terms, says that the new bride is only to relieve Lahana of her menial work, and gives her gold for ornaments which have always a magic effect in comforting and composing the female mind. The marriage follows, but the happy pair are not allowed to taste its sweets. The king wishes to have a golden cage for a pet bird, and Dhanapati is ordered to go to Eastern Bengal where such articles were manufactured. Dhanapati leaves his village in the District of Burdwan, leaving his new wife Khullana to the tender mercies of her fellow-wife Lahana.

For some time the two wives live in peace, but as often happens in Hindu families, a female servant foments their jealousies and arouses their hatred towards each other. Durbala, a character very powerfully drawn, repairs to the elder wife Lahana, discourses on the beauty of Khullana, and impresses on Lahana that Dhanapatti will neglect her on his return. Such insinuations arouse Lahana's jealousy, and after some subterfuges she has a letter forged, purporting to come from Dhanapati, and directing that Khullana should be employed in tending goats. Khullana is no patient Griselda, for Mukunda Ram never paints characters with superhuman virtues or vices. Khullana, though the heroine of the poem, is like any ordinary woman of flesh and blood, and it is no part of the poet's scheme to represent her as possessed of extraordinary patience or virtue. She falls out with her fellow-wife, and even returns her taunts and blows.

Khullana however succumbs at last, and consents to take out her husband's goats every day to the fields to graze. With a heavy heart and bitter tears she goes through this unaccustomed and humiliating task, and the account of her long sufferings and sorrows and of her wanderings in fields and jungles, her soliloquies and addresses to birds, her sleep and her dream of her mother,—these are among the most affecting passages in the work.[5]

[5]We make a few extracts here :—

khullanā chāgal rākhe pāp jyaiṣṭha māse|
agnisama aṅga poḍe ravir prakāśe||
* * * *
bhādare carāy cheli bhije sarva gā|
* * * *
tuṣār śital ṛtu him cāri mās|
khullanār śit khaṇḍe ravir prakāś||
* * * *

It was for a *Suk* bird that her husband went to East Bengal to procure a golden cage, and Khullana bursts forth into an exclamation of grief on seeing a pair of *Suk* birds on the tree :

sārī śuyā tumi dile etek yātanā|
āsi rājā vidyamān piñjare sādhite mān
anāthinī karile khullanā||
gauḍ gelā prāṇanāth cheli rākhi khāi bhāt
parite nā mile paridhān|
* * * *
tomāre dhariyā śuk ghucāva maner dukh
ekākinī sārī yena kānde||
* * * *

Khullana makes a familiar exclamation on seeing some bees collecting honey from flowers :—

bhramarī bhramar toye yudi kar
nā gāo madhur gīt|
* * * *
saṅge tor vadhū pān kare madhu
ki kava sukher or|
anāthī dekhiyā tor nāhi dayā
citta haila mor cor||
* * * *
tor saṅge alinī nirās nalinī
nā jāna viraha-vyathā|

Chandi at last comes to the rescue of Khullana. She appears to Lahana in a vision and upbraids her, and Lahana repents, embraces Khullana as her sister, and relieves her of her humiliating work. Soon after Dhanapati, who like an easy-going, pleasure-loving man was leading a life of pleasure in Eastern Bengal, returns to his country with the golden cage, and who is so happy as the young and beauteous Khullana, the darling of her husband?

We shall not dwell on the joy of the young wife on the return of her husband; nor on the schemes of Durbala who, true to her character, goes first to congratulate Khullana with *ār śunecha choṭa mā sādhu āila ghare* &c., and then to Lahana to foment her anger and jealousy with *ār śunecha baḍa mā satār carit* &c. Then follows a graphic account of Durbala's bringing things from the market and the young wife cooks them with skill of a *chéf de cuisine* to please her husband. Lahana attempts to conceal her cruelty towards Khullana by many specious excuses, and vainly tries to dissuade Khullana from going to her lord. Needless it is to dwell on the raptures of the meeting between Dhanapati and Khullana who appears in superb dress and beauty, recounts her sufferings, but forgets them all in the embraces of her lord.

But there is no rest for the merchant. The king is in

citta camakita yadi yāo gita
khāo bhramarir māthā||

* * * *

Khullanā's address to the kokil deserves to be quoted :—

kokil he kata ḍāka sulalita rā|
madhu-svare divāniśi nitya ugāra riṣi
virahi janer poḍe gā||

* * * *

ke tomāre kahe bhāla bhitare rāhire kāla
vadh kaile anāth yuvati||

* * * *

sadāgar āche yathā kena nāhi yāo tathā
ei vane ḍāka akāraṇ||
āsiyā vasantakāle rasiyā rasāl ḍāle
prati din deyasi yantraṇā|
hena lay mor mane āsi kira ei sthāne
pikarūpī haila lahanā||

want of some spices, and Dhanapati must again leave his home and his young wife, then with child. and sail to Ceylon for the spices. Going down the Ajay river, the vessel comes to the modern Hugli River, and successively passes by Nabadwip, Santipur, Tribeni, and then comes into the boisterous Meghna. There a storm arises and destroys most of the boats. The merchant then comes into the land of the Firingis (Portuguese) whom the poet has described in very uncomplimentary language. After this the merchant must come out into the open sea, and the poet's notions of geography become somewhat hazy, for he makes his hero pass first through a sea of prawns and lobsters, then through a sea of crabs, then through one of snakes, then of alligators, then of cowries, then of conches! Anyhow the merchant at last manages to come to Setubandha and thence to Ceylon. In the adjacent seas Dhanapati sees, through the deception of Chandi, a marvellous sight, *viz.,* that of a damsel of superb beauty sitting on a lotus and swallowing an elephant! He narrates this story to the King of Ceylon who takes him to be a liar and an impostor and imprisons him, and so ends his adventure.

At Ujjaini, Khullana has a son whom she names Sripati or Srimanta. In course of time the infant grows up to a boy, and with other boys goes to the village pathsala. One day, the guru gets angry with Srimanta, and taunts him in very vulgar terms in reference to the absence of his father. The boy returns home, and though of tender years, resolves on going in quest of his father. All persuasion is vain, the boy has the determination of a man, and he has made up his mind.

Poor Khallana has not the heart to let her son go to that distant region from whose bourne his father had not returned; but Chandi comes down, consoles the distressed mother, and promises to take special care of the son. Srimanta Sudagar sets sail, and in due time reaches Ceylon after witnessing the strange damsel on the lotus whom his father had seen. He repeats the story to the King of Ceylon who orders him to be executed for telling a lie. Poor Srimanta is led to the place of execution. but still remains unaltered in his faith towards Chandi, whom he addresses in the thirty-four consonants of the Bengali alphabet,—an address which Bharat Chandra has imitated in his Bidya Sundar. The goddess descends in the shape of an old Brahman woman, and ultimately rescues Srimanta after beating back the whole force of the king. The king at last discovers Chandi and worships her, honours her protege Srimanta, and promises to bestow his daughter Susila on him. But Srimanta is disconsolate, and will not marry till he sees his father. At his request the king releases all the prisoners, and they are one by one provided with money and things and sent home. The heart of the child throbs at the sight of his father whom he has never seen before, and the old man gives a true account of himself to the young Srimanta, little knowing that it is his own son he is speaking to. Srimanta still remains incognito, and hands over the last will and testament which his father had left with Khullana before leaving home. Affecting is the passage in which the old man, on seeing the letter, suddenly recollects his distant home and cries out in bitter grief. The son discovers himself, and they both return home to the bosom of their family.

Such are the plots of Mukunda Ram's poems; with regard to the merits of his poetry we have said much already. Its most remarkable feature is its intense reality. Many of the incidents are superhuman and miraculous, but the thoughts and feelings and sayings of his men and women are perfectly natural, recorded with a fidelity which has no parallel in the whole range of Bengali literature.

The characters of Mukunda Ram, too, are not princes and princesses, but men and women in the ordinary ranks of life, a hunter of low caste and his wife, a trader and his two wives. The poet has no ordinary powers of character-painting. All the pictures he has drawn are from life; and often, without almost intending it, he hits off in a few lines a character, clear and distinguishable from all others. Kalaketu is a boorish, strong, brave and simple-minded hunter, Fullara a poor dutiful wife, Murari Sil an astute shop-keeper, Bharu Datta an impudent and pretending impostor, Dhanapati an ease-loving, easy-going, elderly, well-to-do trader, Lahana and Khullana are rival wives. with all the faults and angry passions of rival wives. and Durbala is a scheming old servant, with all the mischievousness and self-importance of old servants in Hindu households.

Pathos is a strong point in Mukunda Ram's writings. A sufferer himself, he has a ready sympathy for all sufferers; and poor Fullara and poor Khullana are not ordinary sufferers. Mukunda Ram's language is flowing, perspicuous and musical, and a quiet humour pervades his poetry.

CHAPTER XI

Ram Prasad and his Songs
(Eighteenth Century)

It is possible to be a true poet without being a great poet, and Ram Prasad Sen is a true poet, every inch of him. In his life and acts, no less than in his songs, the poet predominates over the man.

Raja Krishna Chandra Rai of Nadia will always figure in the annals of Bengali literature as a liberal and enlightened parton of learning. The court of Krishna Chandra was an assemblage of poets and learned Brahmans. Of these, two have left their names and works to posterity. Ram Prasad Sen and Bharat Chandra Rai are the two great poets of the eighteenth century.

Ram Prasad Sen, a Vaidya by caste, was born in Kumarhatta in Halishar in the district of Nadia, probably about 1720. He was the son of Ram Ram Sen, and the grandson of Ramesvara Sen; and he had a son named Ram Dulal, and a daughter named Jagadisvari.

In early life he went to Calcutta as a Sarkar or agent of a well-to-do citizen; but like Frank Osbaldistone, he field his ledger books with poetry, and composed songs when he should have cast up accounts. The Head Sarkar took offence at this gross breach of all rules and precedents, and took the trembling young poet and his account books to his master. The latter, however, very unlike the elder Osbaldistone, appreciated the talent of the young novice; and what was the surprise of the old Sarkar when the master, instead of reproving the bad accountant, admired the true poet. and sent him back to his native village on a pension of 30 Rupees per mensem. It is seldom that men of business appreciate talent so quickly or honour genius so handsomely. We transcribe the song which is said to have specially charmed the young accountant's master. It is a song addressed to the goddess Kali. and clothed in metaphor, as Ram Prasad's songs generally are.[1]

Ram Prasad, once more in his native village, gave full vent to his talent for songs. He had no work to do, no cares and anxieties to disturb his peace. Life for him was as a sweet poem,—one sweet song full of pathos and feeling. He was a Tantrika, a devout worshipper of Kali, and he was careless of this world, and lived in his faith in Kali. Kali or Sakti, Durga or Chandi. is not an unapproachable deity; she is the ideal of a Hindu mother, tender and loving beyond expression, ministeiing to every want and helpful in every difficulty. In her illimitable love she must put up even with the reproaches of her wayward sons; and the songs to Kali are oftener complaints of her cruelty than thanksgivings for her mercy. Most of the songs of Ram Prasad relate to Kali, and it is impossible to convey to the English reader any thing of the pathos and the tenderness with which the poet appeals to his deity, or rather the child appeals to his mother. In this consists the beauty, the simplicity, the sweetness of Ram Prasad's songs. a sweetness so overpowering, that even to the present day the listener is affected by them as the very beggars of our towns sing the strains of Ram Prasad from street to street.

The fame of Ram Prasad Sen spread from day to day, till at last Raja Krishna Chandra Rai of Nadia heard of him, and welcomed him, and listened to his songs. To know the poet was to admire him. to know the man was to like him, and Ram Prasad soon rose in the Raja's favour. He rewarded him with the title of Kabiranjan, and with the more substantial gift of a 100 bighas of rent-free land. In return, Ram

[1] āmāy dāo mā tasildārī |
āmi nemak-hārām nai śaṅkari||
pada ratna bhāṇḍār savāi luṭe ihā āmi sahite nāri|
bhāṇḍār jimmā āchhe yār se ye bholā tripurāri||
śiv āśutoṣ svabhāv dātā tavu jimmā rākha tāṁri |
ardha aṅga jāygīr tabu śiver māinā bhāri ||
āmi vinā māiner cākar keval caraṇ-dhūlār adhikārī
yadi tomār vāper dhārā dhara tabe vaṭe āmi hāri;
yadi āmār vāper dhārā dhārā tabeta mā pete pāri||
prasād bale eman pader vālāi laye āmi mari|
'o pader mata pad pāi to se pad laye vipad sāri||

Prasad wrote a poem on the well-known story of Bidya Sundar. and dedicated it to the Raja. We must admit, this work is disappointing to the reader. It was not in Ram Prasad's line to write long narrative poems, and his attempt was a failure. Probably too his anxiety to make the present commensurate with the kindness of the Raja hampered him in his composition. We may therefore dismiss this subject with the remark, that the *Bidya Sundar* of Ram Prasad is generally stiff and artificial, but shews a thorough mastery of an alliterative though somewhat artificial style.[2]

Several stories are told about Ram Prasad. It is said he went to Murshidabad with Raja Krishna Chandra, and sang to the Raja in a boat on the Hugli. The boat of Nawab Surajuddawla passed that way, and the Subahdar was pleased with Ram Prasad's songs, got him into his own boat. and commanded him to sing. Ram Prasad sang in Hindi, but the Subahdar would have none of it. and ordered Ram Prasad to sing the same songs he had sung just before. The poet did so, and it is said, the Subahdar was charmed with the performance.

A curious story is told of Ram Prasad's death. On the last day of the Kali Puja, when the Hugli was covered with boats carrying the images of Kali, Ram Prasad became unusually excited. He sang of Kali till, by one account, he jumped from his boat into the river and was drowned, or by another account, he fell down in a swoon and died.

We quote below a few of the most popular songs of Ram Prasad.[3]

[2]Bidyā's lament on the apprehension of Sundar.

kona dharma hena karma poḍe marme gātra-carma
diyā diva pādukā caraṇe|
hṛdayeś ei reś pāye kleś kṛpa leś
kara bhāi akāl maraṇe||

The Queen's lament on the detection of her daughter's frailty.

nahe sukhī sumukhī nirakhi nandinīre|
asambar ambar ambar paḍe śire||

The Queen's address to the King.

śire hāni pāṇi rāṇi bale kara ki|
śura parva garva kharva garbhavati jhī||

[3] *man kṛṣi-kāj tor ese nā*
eman mānav-janam railo paḍe ārād karle phalta soṇā|

One great charm of his poetry consists in the simple homely similes, always drawn from familiar objects of lowly village life. The cultivated rice-field, the ferry boat, the village market, the oil-mill, such are the objects of his similes. round which he entwines his feeling songs with the most touching effect.

The eighteenth century produced many other poets in Bengal, and Ghanaram's voluminous work, written early in the century, has recently been published. But Ghanaram and other poets like him are little known to the reading public of Bengal. The songs of Ram Prasad and the poetry of Bharat Chandra are the greatest literary products of this century.

guru ropaṇ karechen bīj tāy bhakti-vāri sece denā|
ore eklā yadi nā checte pāris rāmprasād ke ḍeke nenā||

*   *   *   *

nitānta yave din edin yāve keval ghoṣaṇā rave go|
tārā name asaṅkhya kalaṅka have go|
esechilām bhaver hāṭe hāṭ kare vasecchi ghāṭe
oma śrīsūrya calila pāṭe nāye lave go|

*   *   *   *

mā āmāy ghurāvi kata|
kalur cokh ḍhākā balader mata|
beṅdhe diye bhaver gāche mā pāk ditecha avirata|
ekvār khule de mā cokher ṭhuli heri tor ai abhaypada||

CHAPTER XII

BHARAT CHANDRA ROY
(EIGHTEENTH CENTURY)

CONTEMPORANEOUSLY with Ram Prasad Sen, and equally favoured by Raja Krishna Chandra Rai, lived a more skilful poet, the talented Bharat Chandra Roy,—a "mine of talent" or *Gunakar*,—as the Raja called him.

Bharat Chandra Roy was the fourth son of Raja Narendra Narain Roy, a Zemindar of Burdwan. The seat of his zemindari was at Pandua in the Pargana of Bhursut, and his residence was surrounded on all sides by a moat, traces of which are visible to the present day. Narendra Narain had disputes with Kirti Chandra Roy, Raja of Burdwan, and made insulting allusions with reference to Kirti Chandra's mother. The queen mother was incensed, and sent an army which attacked and took the forts of Bhabanipur and Pandua, and desolated the states of Narendra Narain. Narendra Narain was reduced to penury, and his young son Bharat Chandra fled for shelter to the house of his maternal uncle at Nawapara, near Gazipur, in the Pargana of Mandalghat. There he studied grammar and dictionary, and at the age of fourteen returned to his native village, and married a girl of the village Sarada. The match was considered dishonourable, and Bharat Chandra's elder brothers reproved him for it. The future poet left his home in disgust, and took shelter with one Ram Chandra Munshi, a Kayastha inhabitant of Debanandpur near Bansbaria in the district of Hugli, and there commenced the study of Persian.

The first poems that Bharat Chandra published to the world were composed under curious circumstances. Bharat Chandra was asked to read hymns to Satya Narain on a certain occasion by the people with whom he lived. The festive day came, and how great was the surprise of the people when, instead of reading the verses usually read on such occasions, he read out *tripadi* verses specially composed by him for the occasion. How much greater was their astonishment when on being asked to chant verses again a few days after on a similar occasion, he read out a new set of *chaupadi* verses which he had composed afresh on the same subject. The poet was then only fifteen.

At the age of twenty Bharat returned home, and as he was well versed in the Persian language, he went over to the court of the Raja of Burdwan, as a Muktear or agent for his brothers for their joint estate.

Bharat's brothers however failed to remit rent in due time, and the Raja, actuated probably by his old grudge against the family, confiscated the estate and took it over as his *khas* lands. Bharat was imprudent enough to protest. and he was imprisoned. Poor Bharat Chandra was now in utter misery, but he did not lose heart. He bribed the jailor and escaped, and at once fled to Cuttack, where he lived under patronage of Siva Bhatta the Mahratta Subahdar of the place. Cuttack, as our readers know, has always been a great stronghold of the Vaishnavas. and in their company Bharat turned a Vaishnava and assumed the dress and demeanour of the sect. Shortly after, while on his journey to Brindaban, he was surprised by some of his distant relatives at Khanakul Krishnagar. As rigid Hindus, they were shocked at the conversion of the poet. They prevented him from going to Brindaban, and after much persuasion made him forsake his Vaishnava dress, and Bharat was a Hindu householder once more. The readers of *Annada Mangal* know that in describing the double conversion of Vyasa, who first became a Vaishnava and then a Sakta or Saiva, the poet has partly explained and partly apologized for his own conduct.

After a short residence at his father-in-law's house at Sarada, Bharat Chandra went over to Chandranagar, where Indra Narain Pal Chaudhuri, Dewan of the French Government, received him with honour. This Pal Chaudhuri was a friend of Raja Krishna Chandra of Nadia, and used to lend him money. On one occasion, when Raja Krishna Chandra came to Chandranagar, Indra Narain introduced the poet to him. The Raja was pleased with the young poet, took him over to Krishnaghar, and appointed him as a Pandit of his court on a monthly pay of 40 Rs. He was pleased with the short pieces which the poet now and then composed.

and asked him to compose a long poem, *Annada Mangal*, after the style of Mukuda Ram's *Chandi*. Bharat composed the poem, and a Brahman of the name of Nilmani Samaddar set it to music, and sang it before the Raja in parts as it was composed. At the request of the Raja the tale of *Bidya Sundar* was subsequently embodied in the work. Krishna Chandra was so pleased with the poet that he made him a grant of 100 Rs. to enable him to build a house at Mulajor which village he leased to the poet on a rent of Rs. 600 per annum.

Shortly afterwards, an incursion of the Mahrattas compelled Raja Tilak Chandra Rai of Burdwan to flee with his mother to Kangachi near Mulajor, and they took *patni* lease of the village from the Raja of Krishnaghar in the name of a servant Ram Deb Nag. This Nag proved to be an oppressive Patnidar. and Bharat Chandra took a poet's revenge in a set of Sanskrit verses entitled the "Nagashtaka" or the eight verses on Nag. The Raja was so pleased with this performance that he made over to Bharat Chandra 16 Bighas at Mulajor and 150 Bighas at Ghusti *rent-free*, intending that Bharat should remove to the latter place if he chose. But Bharat's co-villagers would not allow him to leave, and Bharat continued to live at Mulajor. Bharat died at the age of 48, in the year 1760.

Critics have formed very different estimates of Bharat Chandra's poetical powers. Many of our countrymen of the old school would place him in the highest rank of poets. but we are unable to share this opinion. Bharat Chandra with all his gifts is but an imitator of Mukunda Ram, and we confess that Bharat Chandra's artificial and polished strains strike us as lifeless, when compared with the simple and faithful pictures from nature. with which Mukunda Ram's works are replete. Mukunda Ram draws from nature. Bhasat Chandra daubs his pictures with gorgeous colours. Bharat Chandra is the more polished and artificial poet, Mukunda Ram is the truer painter and the greater poet.

That Bharat Chandra has his beauties, none will deny. His three works *Annada Mangal. Bidya Sundar*, and *Mansinha* form one continuous story, and are in reality but one work. Like Mukunda Ram, Bharat Chandra intends to glorify the name and deeds of the goddess Uma or Chandi, and instead of narrating the story of an imaginary hero, he has taken up the story of the life of Bhabanand Mazumdar. the renowned ancestor of his patron and benefactor, Raja Krishna Chandra Rai of Nadia. The poet begins with an account of the birth of Uma, the great feast given by Daksha to which Siva was not invited, the self-immolation of Uma in consequence, her second birth as daughter of the Himalayas, her marriage with Siva, and other mythological stories with which every Hindu is familiar. The poet's rare power of graceful versfication enable him to tell these stories with effect, the reader peruses page after page with the same sense of pleasure. and at times he is struck with passages in which the poet shews a keen sense of humour. Such, for instance, is the description of Siva's marriage, and such again is the account of his disputes with his young wife. We need scarcely remind our readers, however, that in all these descriptions Bharat is a close imitator of Mukunda Ram.

We need not stop to narrate how the great poet and saint, Vyasa, quarrelled with Siva. and made an abortive attempt to build up a new Benares to rival the town of Benares where Siva is worshipped by all. We pass over all this, and at last find Uma on her way to the house of Bhabanand Mazumdar. She has to cross a stream, and the account she gives of herself to the ferryman is justly regarded as remarkable specimen of artistic poetry. The whole passage[1] may be interpreted in two different ways, and while the ferryman understands her to be the neglected wife of a Kulin Brahman who has many other wives, the goddess obscurely gives a true account of herself. Our readers will perceive that this passage is only an imitation of a similar ingenious passage

[1] A few typical lines are quoted here—Editor.

íśvarīre paricay kahen isvarī|
bujhaha īsvarī āmi paricay karī||

* * * *

gotrer pradhān pitā mukha-vamśa-jāta|
param kulīn svāmī vandya-vamśa-khyāta||

* * * *

gaṅgā nāme satā tār taraṅga emani|
jīvan-svarūpā se svāmīr śiromaṇi||

* * * *

in Mukunda Ram's work; but we confess the imitation is superior to the original both in grace and in art, for Bharat is superior to Mukunda Ram in art. Uma at last reaches the house of Bhabanand Mazumdar. and from that day the house rises in glory and importance. Pratap Aditya Rai, a refractory Zemindar of Jessore Iswaripur, defies the power of the Emperor Aurungzeb, and the renowned Man Sinha is sent to quell the chief. That warrior finds some difficulty in carrying his forces over the swamps and marshes of Southern Bengal, and Bhabanand renders him signal assistance. At last a battle is fought of which we have a spirited though somewhat grotesque description, and Pratap Aditya is killed. It is when Bhabanand is accompanying Man Sinha in his marches that he narrates to the Rajput chief the story of *Bidya Sundar;* so that that story is not a portion of the main plot in any way.

In the story of Bidya Sundar the poet has tried to cast a stain on the Raj family of Burdwan, and his early disputes with that family must have impelled him to the task. The German poet Heine sings :

> Affront the living poets not,
> With weapons and flames they are furnished.

And Bharat Chandra has certainly revenged himself on the house of Burdwan with his direct weapons in his story of *Bidya Sundar.* The story is that of a princess of the Burdwan house, who falls in love with a young prince from Southern India who has come to Burdwan in disguise. The young prince secures the services of an astute flower-woman whose character has been powerfully drawn by the poet,[2]

[2] *sūrya yāy astagiri āise yāminī|*
henakāle tathā ek āilā māline||
kathāy hīrār dhār hīrā tār nām|
dant cholā mājā dolā hāsa avirām||
* * * *
āchila vistar ṭhāṭ pratham vayase|
eve buḍā tabu kichu guṅḍā āche śeṣe||
chiṭā phoṭā mantra tantra āse kataguli|
ceṅgḍā bhulāye khāy kata jāne ṭhuli||
* * * *

although it is only an imitation, and not an improved, one, of Mukunda Ram's Durbala.

The flower woman takes an epistle of love curiously woven by the foreign prince in a garland to the princess, and the effect which follows is described, as only Bharat Chandra can describe such subjects.[3]

Other incidents follow, and the prince Sundar at last finds admission into the appartments of the languishing princess Bidya. The descriptions which folow are repugnant to modern taste, and have left a stain on Bharat Chandra's poetry and fame. Bidya's frailty is soon discovered, and the anger of the queen mother at her daughter's misconduct is powerfully described.[4] At last the young prince is detected

[3] *śuna go mālini ki tor rīti|*
kiñcit hṛdaye nā hay bhīti||
* * *
buk bāḍiyāche kār sohāge|
kāli śikhāiva māyer āge||
buḍā hali tabu nā gela ṭhat|
rāṅḍ haiye yena sāṅḍer nāṭ||
* * *
hirā thara thara kāñpiche ḍare|
tomār kāje ki nayane jhare||
* * *
cikaṇ gāthane bāḍila velā|
tomār kaje ki āmār helā||
* * *
vinayete vidyā haila vaś|
asta gela roṣ uday ras||
* * *

[4] *krodhe rāṇī dhāy rade añcal dharōy pade*
āluthālu kabarī-bandhan|
* * * *
raṇī āila krodhamane nūpurer jhanjhane
uṭhe vaise virsiṁha rāy||
* * * *
rāṇī bale mahārāj ki kava kahite lāj
kalaṅke pūrila sav deś||
* * * *
ghare dibaḍa meye kakhana nā dekha ceye
vivāher nā bhāva upāy|
anāyāse pāve sukh dekhive nātir mukh
eḍāile jhīr viyā dāy||
* * * *

and ordered to be excuted. But the goddess Kali interferes and saves the offender from his well-merited punishment, even as Mukunda Ram's Chandi saves Srimanta Sadagar when the King of Ceylon orders his execution.

Bharat Chandra's style is always rich, graceful and flowing. Nowhere perhaps in the entire range of Bengali literature do we find the language of poetry so rich, so graceful, so overpowering in artistic beauty as in *Bidya Sundar.* He is a complete master of the art of versification, and his appropriate phrases and rich descriptions have passed into bye-words. It would be difficult to overestimate the polish he has given to the Bengali language.

Another feature of Bharat Chandra's poetry is the vividness of his descriptions. As the descriptions are not always of a healthy character, the reader regrets that they are so vivid, but nevertheless confesses the power of the poet. In character-painting however, Bharat Chandra cannot be compared with the great master whom he has imitated. Fullara and Khullana are women of flesh and blood with distinct characters; in Bidya we can discover no trait of character except a capacity for voluptuous love. Durbala and Bharu Datta are powerfully-drawn portraits from life; Hira Malini is an over-drawn caricature. And in all the higher qualifications of a poet, in truth, in imagination, and even in true tenderness and pathos, such as we meet with in almost every other Bengali poet, Bharat Chandra is singularly and sadly wanting.

Bharat Chandra died three years after the battle of Plassey. New actors now entered on the stage; and new influences shaped the course of the literature of Bengal in the nineteenth century.

uccamāthā haila heṭ vidyār hayeche peṭ
kālamukh dekhāibe kāre||

*   *   *   *

vidyār ki diva doṣ tāre vṛthā kari roṣ
viyā haile haita kata chele|
yauvane kāmer jvālā kadin sahibe bālā
kathāy rākhiva kata ṭhele||

CHAPTER XIII

Ram Mohan Roy and his religious reform
(1774-1833)

We now enter upon the brightest period in the annals of Bengali literature. The British Conquest of Bengal was not merely a political revolution, but brought in a greater revolution in thought and ideas, in religion and social progress. The Hindu intellect came in contact with all that is nobelest and most healthy in European history and literature, and profited by it. The Hindu mind was to some extent trained under the influence of European thoughts and ideas, and benefited by it.

Towards the close of the last century, Warren Hastings compiled Hindu and Muhammadan laws for the use of courts, and associated Pandits and Maulavis with European Judges for the administration of justice. This was the first intellectual contact between Europeans and the best educated natives of Bengal. In 1799 Carey, Ward and Marshman began their missionary work in Serampore and established a Bengali press; they printed the Mahabharata, the Ramayana, and other Bengali works; and they even started a Bengali newspaper. In 1800 Lord Wellesley established the Fort William College for the training of young civilians in the languages of India, secured the services of the most learned Pandits, and encouraged the compilation of vernacular works. Sir William Jones, Colebrooke and Wilson prosecuted researches into the untrodden field of Sanscrit learning and Indian antiquities; they received the help of Hindu Pandits; and they excited in the people of India an interest in their past literature and history. David Hare, a watchmaker in Calcutta, but a man of strong common sense and philanthropy, initiated English education in Bengal, and eventually helped in the establishment of the Hindu College in 1817. Richardson and Derozio were sympathetic teachers, and inspired in the young students of the Hindu College a passionate admiration for English literature and English institutions. And lastly, the great Macaulay advocated in his historic minute that higher education should be imparted to the people of India through the English language and Lord William Bentinck closed his beneficent administration in 1835 by ratifying this minute, and placing English education in India on a solid foundation. These are, briefly, some of the steps by which English education and European influence have spread in Bengal in the present century.

Ram Mohan Roy was the first brilliant product of European influence in India. He was born at Radhanagar in the District of Hugli in 1774, the year in which Warren Hastings became the first Governor General of India, and the Supreme Court was established. The story of the life and work of the great reformer would fill a volume; it is the story of the social, moral and intellectual progress of the Hindus during the first thirty years of this century. The great controversies in which he engaged, first with his countrymen and then with Christian missionaries, mark the awakening of a new life in India. The pure and monothestic Hindu faith which he preached, and the church which he established, flourish to the present day. And the numerous works which he published, in English and in Bengali, have now been compiled and placed in a collected form before his admiring countrymen. The venerable Raj Narayan Basu, himself a writer of merit and distinction, has done a signal service to the cause of Bengali literautre by publishing the Bengali works of Raja Ram Mohan Roy. And later still, the English works of the great reformer have been edited and publised in two stout octavo volumes by Jogendra Chandra Ghosh and Isan Chandra Basu. Our countrymen are grateful to them for this patriotic task; but a proper biography of the great reformer has yet to be written. We can, within our limits, only narrate a few leading facts relating to his life and works.

Ram Mohan's father was Ram Kanta Roy, a petty Zemindar, who had served under the Nawabs of Murshidabad, and had witnessed their fall. And Ram Mohan's mother was Tarini Debi, a woman of great piety and remarkable firmness of character,—virtues which descended from mother to son.

Hindu boys, ambitious of obtaining employment, used

to learn Bengali and Persian in those days; and Ram Mohan acquired a knowledge of both the languages in his native village, and was then sent to Patna in his ninth year to learn Arabic. With his remarkable intelligence, young Ram Mohan mastered the Persian and Arabic languages in three years, and then proceeded to Benares to study Sanscrit. This was the turning point of Ram Mohan's life; It was in Benares that the young man not only mastered the Sanscrit language, but also acquired a knowledge of the noble tenets of the *Upanishads* and the *Vedanta,* which he made it his life's work to preach and proclaim to his countrymen.

After completing his education Ram Mohan returned to his native village, and at the early age of sixteen, in the year 1790, he wrote his famous work on the Idolatrous Religion of the Hindus (*Hindudiger pauttalik dharmapraṇālī*) which is the first literary work in Bengali prose that we know of. For while Bengali Poetry had flourished in the previous centuries, there was no such thing as a prose literature in Bengali. Raja Ram Mohan Roy is the *father of prose literature in Bengal.*

Ram Mohan's father was grieved and offended at the publication of the young reformer's early work,[1] and Rom Mohan had to leave his paternal home, and spent his time in travels.[2] It is said he penetrated into Tibet and remained for three years, studying Buddhism. His father now relented and called back his son to his home, and Ram Mohan began the study of the English language when he was 22 years of age. With his extraordinary intellect and his keen desire for learning he not only learnt English so as to be able to write that language correctly, fluently and forcibly, but he also acquired some knowledge of French and Latin, and it is said, of Greek and Hebrew also.

[1] We regret we do not find this first work of Ram Mohan Roy in the collection of his works published by Raj Narayan Basu.

[2] Ram Mohan Roy himself wrote of this in an autobiographical sketch, addressed to a friend during his stay in England :

"When about the age of sixteen I composed a manuscript calling in question the validity of the idolatrous system of the Hindus. This, together with my known sentiments on that subject, having produced a coolness between me and my immediate kindred, I proceeded on my travels, and passed through different countries, chiefly within, but some beyond the bounds of Hindustan."

At the same time he carried on controversies with Brahmans about idol worship, the burning of widows, and similar subjects.

On the death of his father he obtained an appointment under Government, and rose to be a Dewan or Sheristadar. He was employed for 13 years (1800-1813) in the service of Government, but the routine of official work did not suit his ardent mind, and in 1814 he retired from work and settled down in Calcutta.

He was now fully equipped for the great controversies into which he entered, on the one hand with orthodox Hindus with a view to lead them to the purer faith of their ancestors, and on the other hand with Christian missionaries who wished to replace Hinduism by Christianity in India. Ram Mohan Roy selected for the modern Hindu his true position in the religious world, and he fortified that position by translations from the ancient Upanishads and other Hindu scriptures, which had so long been the monopoly of a few Pandits, and which now came like a surprise and a joy to all thoughtful and pious Hindus.

It is not our purpose to enumerate all the works which proceeded from the great reformer's pen in this, the most eventful period of his life, but it is necessary to mention some of the more important works. Ram Mohan retired from service and settled down in Calcuta, not to rest but to work, and works proceeded from his fertile pen with a rapidity which amazed and bewildered his friends and opponents alike. In 1815, appeared his Bengali rendering of *Vedanta* philosophy, and in the following year he published *Vedanta Sara* and an abridgment in English of that system of philosophy. The spirit, which inspired the pious and indomitable worker is well set forth in the concluding lines of his introduction to this work,—lines which should live in the memory of his countrymen as long as they continue to appreciate courage, honesty of purpose and devotion to duty.

"By taking the path which conscience and sincerity direct, I, born a Brahman, have exposed myself to the complainings and reproaches, even of some of my relations, whose prejudices are strong, and whose temporal advantage depends upon the present system. But these, however accumulated,

I can tranquilly bear, trusting that a day will arrive, when my humble endeavours will be viewed with justice, perhaps acknowledged with gratitude. At any rate, whatever men may say, I cannot be deprived of this consolation: my motives are acceptable to that Being who beholds in secret and compensates openly."

The 1816 and 1817, he translated several *Upanishads* into Bengali and into English, and in the three following years he published his powerful and famous discourses in Bengali and in English, condemning the burning of widows. As a specimen of Ram Mohan Rai's Bengali prose style, we quote the concluding passage from the first of these essays.[3] Our readers will see that Bengali prose had not yet received the purity and grace which subsequent writers have imparted to it. But Ram Mohan's rugged and well-reasoned style suited the great task he set before himself,—to battle single-handed against a host of unreasoning antagonists, and to expose evil customs and hurtful practices. Raja Radha Kanta Deb headed the orthodox party in those days, defended existing practices, and stood forth against all reform. It was a curious spectacle, that of a Brahman seeking to remove the abuses of modern Hinduism, and a Kayastha standing forth as their champion and defender! The whole orthodox party gathered round Raja Radha Kanta, angry Pandits indulged in

[3]**Prabartak**—*erūp sahamaraṇe o anumaraṇe*
pāp i hauk kimbā yāhā hauk
āmarā e vyavahārke nivarta
karite diva nā ihār nivṛtti
haile haṭhat laukik ek āśaṅkā
āche ye svāmir mṛtyu haile
strī sahagaman nā kariyā vidhavā
avasthāy rahile tāhār vyabhicār
haivār sambhāvanā thāke kintu
sahamaraṇ karile e āśaṅkā
thākenā . . . .

Nibartak—*keval bhābi āśaṅkāke dūr*
karibār nimitte erūp strī-vadhe
pāp jāniyāo nirday haiyā jñān
pūrvak pravarta haiteche tabe
ihāte āmarā ki karite pāri kintu
vyabhicārer āśaṅkā pati vartamān
thākitei vā kon nā āche . . . .

violent attacks and vituperation, and for a time Ram Mohan's life was in danger, and he went about with a guard. But the great and undaunted reformer never swerved one inch from the path he had chosen, and he triumphed over all opposition.

The invincible combatant next turned his arms against the Christian missionaries of Serampore. There is a history connected with his *Precepts of Jesus* and his three *Appeals* which are worth recording. These essays were published between 1820 and 1823, and occupy over five hundred closely printed octavo pages of Ram Mohan's English works. From early youth, Ram Mohan preached monotheism and a pure system of morality, and he was attracted by the teachings of Christ when he came in contact with Christians. In 1820, he published in Sanskrit and in Bengali the *Precepts of Jesus,* separating them "from the abstruse doctrines and miraculous relations of the New Testament." This gave offence to the Serampore missionaries, and a reply appeared in the *Friend of India*, the editor Dr, Marshman adding his own observation and calling Ram Mohan a "heathen."

Ram Mohan published his first and second *Appeals,* in defence of his *Precepts,* and printed them at the Baptist Mission Press, and Dr. Marshman sucessively replied to them. But when Ram Mohan came forward with his third and *Final Appeal,* the Baptist Mission Press refused to print it. Ram Mohan was not to be baffled; he established a press of his own, and published his *Final Appeal* with its formidable array of Hebrew and Greek quotations. Dr. Marshman republished his replies in London, and the Unitarian Society there published Ram Mohan's *Appeals* in 1824, and they were republished in America, in 1828.

The remarkable ability and learning displayed by Ram Mohan were at once acknowledged in Europe and in America. Dr. Carpenter, commenting on the second *Appeal* said, "that the excellent author is distinguished by the closeness of his reasoning, the critical accuracy of his scriptural knowledge, the comprehensiveness of his investigations, the judiciousness of his arrangements, the lucid statements of his opinions, and the acuteness and skill with which he controverts the positions of his opponents."

But it was not the task of controverting the opinions of

his opponents, it was not the task of *destruction*, which Ram Mohan set before himself as the great work of his life. It was the task of *construction*, it was the task of leading back his countrymen to the pure religion of the *Upanishads* and the *Vedanta*, which he set before himself. As early as 1814, immediately after his retirement from the service of Government, Ram Mohan founded the *Atmiya Sabha* for the worship of the One Invisible God of the Upanishads. Later on, he established the *Veda Mandir* for the stüdy of the Vedas. Many pious and prayerful men gathered round him, and the cause of Hindu monotheism prospered in spite of all opposition. And at last, in 1828, he established the Brahmo Samaj, the crowning work of his life, "for the worship and adoration of the Eternal, Unsearchable, Immutable Being who is the Author and Preserver of the Universe." Dwarka Nath Tagore and Prasanna Kumar Tagore[4] helped him, and stood by him in this noble work, and Ram Chandra Vidyabagis was the minister of the Church from the commencement. It was this minister who kept up the church after Ram Mohan's death, until Dwarka Nath's son Devendra nath Tagore accepted the religion of the Brahma Samaj and became its stay and support.

We have so long spoken of Ram Mohan's labours in the cause of religion, for his fame rests mainly on his religious reform. But his keen intellect and encyclopædic mind grasped every question which attracted public attention, and in every question his vast energies were enlisted in the cause of reform. Ram Mohan Roy and David Hare and Sir Edward Hyde East were the prime movers in the founding of the Hindu College in 1817. In 1823 Ram Mohan addressed a letter to Lord Amherst then Governor General, which almost foreshadows Lord Macaulay's famous minute on the merits of Sanscrit and English education.[5] And in the same year

[4] The proper spelling of the name is *Thakur*; but we write it as the members of this cultured family write their names.

[5] We quote the concluding passages of Ram Mohan's letter here. "The Sanscrit system of education would be the best calculated to keep this country in darkness, if such had been the policy of the British legislature. But as the improvement of the native population is the object of the Government, it will consequently promote a more liberal and enlightened system of instruction, embracing Mathematics, Natural Philosophy, Chemis-

we find him, along with Dwarka Nath Tagore and Prasanna Kumar Tagore, appealing to the Supreme Court and then to the throne of England for the liberty of the Press, and thus starting that system of constitutional agitation for political rights which his countrymen have learned to value so much in the present day.

Ram Mohan also wrote on the rights of Hindu females in ancient times, and on other legal questions, but it was his prolonged endeavours to abolish the rite of *Sati* which brought him to prominent notice with the rulers of the country. We have seen that he began the controversy in 1818, and after twelve years of persistent agitation he had the satisfaction of witnessing the triumph of the holy and righteous cause.[6]

try, Anatomy, with other useful sciences, which may be accomplished with the sums proposed by employing a few gentlemen of talent and learning educated in Europe, and providing a College furnished with necessary books, instruments, and other apparatus.

In presenting this subject to your Lordship, I conceive myself discharging a solemn duty which I owe to my countrymen, and also to that enlightened sovereign and legislature which have extended their benevolent care to this distant land, actuated by a desire to improve the inhabitants, and therefore humbly trust you will excuse the liberty I have taken in thus expressing my sentiments to your Lordship."

[6] Raja Radha Kanta Deb, as the leader of the orthodox community, opposed the abolition of Sati. Ram Mohan Roy and his party supported Government on this memorable occasion, and presented an address to Lord William Bentinck after he had suppressed the cruel rite. The reply of the Governor General to this address is worth quoting.

"It is very satisfactory for me to find that, according to the opinions of so many respectable and intelligent Hindus, the practice which has recently been prohibited, not only was not required by the rules of their religion, but was at variance with those writings which they deem to be of the greatest force and authority. Nothing but a reluctance to inflict punishment for acts which might be conscientiously believed to be enjoined by religious precepts, could have induced the British Government at any time to permit, within territories under its protection, an usage so violently opposed to the best feelings of human nature. Those who present this address are right in supposing that by every nation in the world, except the Hindus themselves, this part of their customs has always been made a reproach against them, and nothing so strangely contrasted with the better features of their own national character, so inconsistent with the affections which unite families, so destructive of the moral principles on which society is founded, has ever subsisted

It was thus that Ram Mohan Roy ardently and enthusiastically supported every movement towards reform and towards the regeneration of his country. Never since the days of Chaitanya has Bengal witnessed such intense agitation as during the first quarter of this century. Never has one man attempted and achieved more for his country than Ram Mohan Roy.

The Emperor of Delhi wished to send an agent to England to represent some of his grievances, and he chose Ram Mohan as his agent, and bestowed on him the title of Raja. Raja Ram Mohan had always eagerly wished to visit the western world and gladly seized this opportunity, and he left for Europe in 1830.

His stay in England brought him no rest. His fame had preceded him, and Ram Mohan Roy was requested to give his evidence before the Select Committee of the House of Commons on the Judical and Revenue Systems of India. The masterly essay which he wrote on this subject occupies over a hundered pages of his collected English works. He was also examined on the condition of the native inhabitants of India. and he wrote on the subject of European Colonization of India.

One of his great objects in proceeding to Europe however was to support the abolition of the rite of *Sati* in the House of Commons. He presented the petitions which he had brought with him to the House of Commons and the House of Lords in person, and had the satisfaction of being present when the appeal against the abolition of *Sati* was rejected on the 11th of July, 1832.

Ram Mohan's great acquirements and noble work became known all over England and in other countries of Europe, and his presence was courted in the highest circles and by men of learning. The poet Campbell wrote of him, the antiquarian Rosen consulted him when he was translating the Rig Veda, and the greatest living philosopher of England,

amongst a people in other respects so civilized. I trust that the reproach is removed for ever ; and I feel a sincere pleasure in thinking that the Hindus will thereby be exalted in the estimation of mankind to an extent in some degree proportioned to the repugnance which was felt for the usage which has now ceased."

Jeremy Bentham, received him with open arms, and addressed him as *"intensely admired and dearly beloved collaborator in the service of mankind."*[7]

After a residence of three years in Europe, Raja Ram Mohan Roy died on the 27th September 1833, and his remains were interred in Bristol. A tomb was subsequently erected there by his friend and distinguished countryman Dwaraka Nath Tagore.

We have spoken of Ram Mohan's work in the formation of Bengali prose. Scarcely less eminent are his services in lyrical verse. The reader will scarcely suspect the enthusiastic reformer to be the author of some of the finest and noblest songs which the Bengali language has known.[8] But the reformer had a heart full of tenderness, piety and genuine feeling; and his songs excite the noblest emotions of the human soul. After a lapse of seventy years, the songs of Ram Mohan Roy are still sung in every home in Bengal.

[7] "Your works" wrote Bentham to Ram Mohan, "are made known to me by a book in which I read a style which, but for the name of a Hindu, I should certainly have ascribed to the pen of a superiorly educated and instructed Englishman." And in the same letter, while praising James Mill's great work on the *History of India*, Bentham remarked: "though as to style I wish I could with truth and sincerity pronounce it equal to yours."

[8] One or two specimens are given here :

mane sthir kariyācha ciradin ki sukhe yāve|
jīvan yauvan dhan mān rave samabhāve||
eị āśe tarutale vasiyācha kutūhale|
viṣay kariyā kole jāna nā tyajite have||
are man suna sār divā ante andhakār|
sukhānte duhkheri bhār vahite have||
ataeva avadhāna ye avadhi thāke prāṇa|
brahme kara samādhān nirmal ānanda pāve||

* * * *

mane kara śeṣer se din bhayaṅkar|
anye vākya kave kintu tumi rạve niruttar||

CHAPTER XIV

Isvar Chadnra Gupta and his Satires (1809-1858[1])

Isvar Chandra Gupta was born in the village of Kanchrapara in 1809, and is the earliest Bengali poet of the present century. His poetry forms a connecting link between the old school of Mukunda Ram and Bharat Chandra and the new school of Madhu Sudan and Hem Chandra. Born when the Hindu society was in a transition state, and naturally endowed with a keen humour, he freely ridiculed much that was false and hollow, and also much that was earnest and true, in the movements of his time. As a poet Isvar Chandra does not rank very high, as a satirist he stands first among the writers of Bengal.

Isvar Chandra's poems have lately been published in a collected from with a memoir of the poet's life by the late Bankim Chandra Chatterjea. This work will be our guide in the present chapter.

Isvar Chandra's father was of humble means, and was employed on a pay of eight Rupees a month in a factory close to his native village. Isvar sometimes lived in his village. and sometimes in Calcutta in the house of his maternal uncle. He lost his mother at an early age, and his father married again, much to the disgust of young Isvar. After this event Isvar lived mostly in Calcutta, in the house of his maternal uncle.

The education of the future poet was neglected; he acquired a knowledge of Bengali in Pathshalas, and also learnt a little English. He frequented the house of the Tagore family in Pathuriaghata, and gradually rose to distinction under the patronage of that family. He was married at the age of 15, against his wishes as we are informed, and domestic bliss was not in store for the young pair.

Under the patronage and with the help of the Tagore

[1] 1812-1859. (See Sukumar Sen : *Bāṅgālā Sāhityer Itihās* I, 1948, p. 998).—Ed

family, Isvar Chandra started a journal called *Sambad Prabhakar* in 1830, and the talent and genius of the young editor soon attracted the attention of the literary world to the journal. Among the writers in this journal we see the names of the most distinguished men of the times, like Raja Radha Kanta Deb, Ram Kamal Sen, Hara Kumar Tagore, Prasanna Kumar Tagore, Pandit Jay Gopal Tarkalankar, Pandit Prem Chand Tarkabagish and others.

Isvar Chandra's productions appeared in prose and verse in this journal. He was an imitator of Bharat Chandra's style, but was not a mere imitator. His keen powers of satire are his own, and his verses on society and life and on the events which were traspiring around him, written in a free and easy style, are among the happiest pieces in their way in the whole range of Bengali literature.[2] The poetry is not

[2] A few instances will suffice :—

Iṁrājī navavarṣa

gorār daṅgale giyā kathā kaha heṁse|
ṭhes mere vāso giyā vivider gheṁse||
rāṅgā mukh dekhe vārā ṭene lao hyām|
doṇṭ keyār hinduyāni ḍyām ḍyām ḍyām||

* * * *

kothāy netib leḍi bali śuna save|
paśur svabhāve ār katakāl rave||
dhanya re votalvāsī dhanya lāl jal|
dhanya dhanya vilāter sabhyatār bal||

* * * *

Pouṣ-pārvaṇ

tomār ki ghar pāṇe kichu nāī ṭān|
hāvāter hāte yāy abhāgīr prāṇ||
ki baliba vāp māye kena dila viye|
ek din sukh nāi gharkannā niye||
konao din nā karile saṁsārer kriye|
divāniśi phero śudhu goṁpe tel diye||
save mātra dui gāchā khāḍu chila hāte|
tāhāo diyāchi baṁdha meyetīr bhāte||

* * * *

vadhūr randhane yadi yāy tāhā eṁke|
śāsuḍī nanad kata kathā kay veṁke||

* * * *

Chadma miśanārī

mūrkha haye ghare thāku dharmapath dhare|
kāj nāi iskulete lekhāpaḍā kare||

* * * *

of a very high order, but Isvar Chandra's witty and flowing verse, his satirical hits, and his vivid descriptions were learnt by rote by a large circle of readers, and were the theme of never-ending admiration. No renowned poet appeared in Bengal in the first half of the present century, and Isvar Chandra was the reigning king of the literary world in his day. But the king had his opponents! One Gauri Sankar Bhattacharja started a rival paper, and a battle of verse was waged for some time, marked more by abuse than by wit!

miṣṭabhāṣī śubhrākār miśanārī yata|
āmāder pakṣe tārā dayādharmahata||

* * * *

śūnya kari jananīr hṛday bhāṇḍār|
haraṇ kariyā lay sādher kumār||

* * * *

vidyādān chal kari miśanārī dab|
pātiyāche bhāla ek vidharmer tab||

* * * *

Pāṁṭhā

rasbharā rasamay raser chāgal|
tomār kāraṇe āmi hayechi pāgal||

* * * *

tumi yār peṭe yāo sei puṇyavān|
sādhu sādhu sādhu tumi chāgīr santān||

* * * *

Nīlkardiger atyācār

hole nīl karder anarāri māñjiṣṭāri bhār|
kuin mā, mā, māgo
hole nīl karder anarāri māñjiṣṭāri bhār|
paḍeche sav pāthar rakṣe abhāgā prajār pakṣe
vicāre rakṣe nāi ko ār|

* * * *

kuṭhiyāl vicārkāri lāṭhiyāl sahakārī
rānarer hāte hola kāler khantā
lontā jale cāṣ|

* * * *

Mudakīr yuddha

legeche viṣam yuddha śīkgaṇ saṅge|
regeche iṁrej lok ranaras raṅge||
sejeche agaṇya sainya ki kar vistār|
bejeche jayer ḍaṅkā nāhika nistār||

* * * *

bhegeche sammukh yuddhe nadīpār haye|
megeche āśray puna mitrabhāv laye||

* * * *

In course of time, Isvar Chandra started the monthly *Prabhakar*, teeming with his inexhaustible verse, and also with prose compositions. He wrote the lives of the older Bengali poets, Mukunda Ram, Bharat Chandra, Ram Prasad and others in this journal, and this was the first attempt to complie the biographies of our old writers. The monthly *Prabhakar* became a power in the land, and young writers of talent and genius like Dina Bandhu Mitra and Bankim Chandra, who subsequently rose to fame and distinction, served their first apprenticeship under Isvar Chandra Gupta in the monthly *Prabhakar*.

Isvar Chandra also took part in recitations and musical performances, (*paṁchālī, hālf akḍāi* &c.), which were in fashion in his day, and his ready wit and ready verse were much appreciated. In his last days he turned to more serious works, mostly translations from the Sanscrit like his *Prabodha Prabhakar* and *Bodhendu Bikas*. The extract which we give below[3] from *Bodhendu Bikas* is a fair specimen of Isvar Chandra's prose style. Our readers will observe that Bengali prose was not yet perfect. Isvar Chandra's prose is not as happy and natural as his poetry, but is artificial and alliterative, and somewhat grotesque.

Minor Poets

Among the minor poets who flourished in the first half of this century, one at least deserves mention. Madan Mohan Tarkalankar was a contemporary of Isvar Chandra. He was born in 1815, and was for sometime Professor in the Sanscrit College,

[3] *he jīv sakal/ei saṁsārke anitya jñān kariyā niyatai maraṇke smaraṇ kara, — maner sakal abhimān haraṇ kara, — santoske maner mandire varaṇ kara, — keval ānanda-dvīpe caraṇ kara,— jīvan jīvan-bimbavat, niśvāser prati viśvās nai, ekhani vināś haive, ataev yata pāra tatai satkārya sādhan kara, — indriyagaṇer vaśibhūta haiyā sakāryer satkārya karā ucit hay nā, param premer premik hao, sakaler priya haiyā prem-pāśe sakalke baddha kara*

* * * *

Some of Iswar Chandra's compound words are virtually Sanskrit compounds. The following passage from *Bodhendu Bikas* will illustrate this :—

kena nā tumi eikāle nava nava nayan-vallabh-pallav mañjarī-maṇḍala-maṇḍita nava nava sucārusundar surabhi-phulla-phuladalasuśovita mṛdu mṛdu malayānila-sevita — ....iccha kara।

and subsequently became a Judge-Pandit and then a Deputy Collector. He died in 1885, *i.e.* in the same year with Isvar Chandra Gupta. His *Rasa Tarangini* is a translation into ornate and musical Bengali verse of some Sanscrit verses on love; and his *Vasavadatta* is a Bengali adaptation of the well-known Sanscrit novel of that name by Subandhu.

CHAPTER XV

AKSHAY KUMAR DATTA
(1820-1886)

AKSHAY KUMAR DATTA and Isvar Chandra Vidyasagar were the true successors of Raja Ram Mohan Roy. They inherited his strong enthusiasm for social reform and devoted their lives to the good of their country. And they also perfected the literary prose style of Bengal which was first rudely shaped by Raja Ram Mohan Roy.

Both Akshay Kumar and Isvar Chandra were born in 1820, Akshay Kumar being senior by two months. Both set before themselves the same lofty purpose, *viz.* the moral instruction of the people and the reform of social abuses. Both contributed to the formation of a chaste and dignified literary prose style in Bengali. And both lived to a ripe old age, and have lately been taken away from us, honoured and lamented by the nation. A meritorious biography of Akshay Kumar has been compiled by Mahendra Nath Vidyanidhi, and an equally meritorious life of Vidyasagar has been compiled by Chandi Charan Banerjea. We cordially acknowledge our indebtedness to both these industrious writers.

Akshay Kumar was born in Chupi, near Nabadwip, and was the son of Pitambar Datta. His mother was Dayamayi, a woman who was distinguished alike by her remarkable intelligence and her natural piety; and like Ram Mohan Roy, Akshay Kumar inherited the virtues of his mother. He learned Bengali in his village Pathshala and also picked up a knowledge of Persian; and at the age of ten he came to Kidderpore near Calcutta, where his father was staying.

The story of the early struggles of Akshay Kumar to acquire sound knowledge through the English language is among the most touching episodes of his instructive life. A copy of Pearson's Dialogues on Geography and Astronomy, in English and Bengali, fell into his hands, and the young boy of ten read with intense interest and delight the account of clouds, rain, lightning and thunder, in the Bengali version.

His eager mind was filled with a desire to know more of the secrets and laws of nature, and at this early age Akshay Kumar determined to learn English in order to acquire such knowledge.

After studying with private teachers for some years to little purpose, the enthusiastic boy got himself admitted in a Missionary school at Kidderpur. His father was alarmed, for a Missionary school was, in those days, looked upon with dread. It was at last settled that the intractable boy would reside with a cousin in Calcutta, and attend the Oriental Seminary, a Hindu institution where English was taught. Akshay Kumar was admitted there at the age of sixteen, and virtually commenced his English education at this age; the knowledge of English which he had been able to acquire before this was but nominal.

But poor Akshay Kumar's difficulties were not yet at an end. He could pay no schooling fees for the period of one year, and the penniless boy came to the proprietor, Gaur Mohan Adhya, with tears in his eyes, and asked permission to leave the school, as he could not afford to pay. Gaur Mohan had marked the intelligence and the uprightness of the boy, he took pity on him, and permitted him to pursue his studies without payment of fees.

But a long course of instruction in this institution was not in store for Akshay Kumar. On the death of his father at Benares, he had to leave the school after remaining there for less then three years. His keen desire for knowledge however continued unabated, the study of Natural Science had special attraction for him, and he continued the study after leaving school. And at the age of twenty he began to learn Sanscrit, the knowledge of which befitted him for the great task of his life, the development of Bengali prose literature.

Isvar Chandra Gupta was then the king of the literary world in Bengal, and Akshay Kumar became acquainted with him. On one occasion, Isvar Chandra asked Akshay to translate an article which had appeared in an English daily paper. "But I have never composed anything in Bengali prose," said young Akshay, "how can I translate this"? With his usual kindness for talented young men, the veteran Isvar Chandra encouraged him in the task, and admired his performance when it was done. Such was Akshay Kumar's initiation into the status of a Bengali writer, and henceforth he began to compose articles for the *Prabhakar*.

But such compositions did not pay, and Akshay Kumar had now to seek for means of livelihood. Various friends gave him various advices. One advised him to be a *Daroga,*[1] and Akshay Kumar seriously began studies to qualify himself for such a post. Soon however he turned away from those studies in disgust; the Police Department lost an honest *Daroga,* and Bengal gained the most talented author and enthusiastic reformer of his day! Another friend advised the young man to study law; but Akshay Kumar instinctively felt, it was not the vocation for him. "Laws change from day to day," he said, "what is the good of studying them? I desire to learn the immutable and unchangeable laws of nature which rule the universe."' Thus time rolled on, and eventually, Akshay Kumar discovered his true vocation in life.

The venerable Debendra Nath Tagore had taken up the task of religious reform which Raja Ram Mohan had initiated, and ten years after Ram Mohan's death in England, started the *Tatvabodhini Patrika,* a monthly journal, in 1843. Young Akshay Kumar, then only a youth of 23, became the editor of the paper which soon became a power in the land. It is scarcely possible in the present day, when journals have multiplied all over the country, to adequately describe how eagerly the moral instructions and earnest teachings of Akshay Kumar, conveyed in that famous paper, were perused by a large circle of thinking and enlightened readers. People, all over Bengal, awaited every issue of that paper with eagerness, and the silent and sickly but indefatigable worker at his desk swayed for number of years the thoughts and opinions of the thinking portion of the people of Bengal. Scientific articles, moral instructions, accounts of different nations and tribes, stories of the animate and inanimate creation, all that could enlighten the expanding intellect of Bengal and dispel darkness and pejudices, found a convenient vehicle in the *Tatvabodhini Patrika.* The great *Prabhakar,* conducted with all the ability and wit of the veteran Isvar Chandra Gupta, continued

[1] Sub-inspector of Police.—Ed.

to be a favourite with orthodox Hindus of the old school. But the *Patrika* was conducted in a newer style, and struck a deeper cord in the heart of the young Hindu. It created a thirst for knowledge and moral elevation, it awakened in rising generations a moral enthusiasm and a religious fervour, and it spread that spirit of reform and of progress of which Raja Ram Mohan Roy was the first great apostle in this century. The profound thought and the earnest tone of Akshay Kumar's writings struck even those who were intensely partial to English education in those days. It is said that the talented Ram Gopal Ghosh, one of the most brilliant students of the Hindu College, read one of Akshay Kumar's articles, and turning to his friend, the distinguished Ram Tanu Lahiri, remarked;—"Have you ever seen profound and thoughtful composition in the Bengali language? It is here."

For twelve years, Akshay Kumar worked indefatigably for this paper. He formed a style of Bengali prose which for elevation, dignity and moral earnestness, has never been surpassed. He wrote articles some of which have since been separately collected and published, and are his best known works, like *Charupatha* and *Dharmaniti*. And for twelve years he was the apostle and the teacher of the party of progress and reform in Bengal. But nature could sustain no longer, and Akshay Kumar was prostrated by a disease of the head.

While Akshay Kumar distinguished himself by his writings in the *Tatvabodhini*, the venerable Vidyasagar also made his mark in literature by works, the like of which Bengal had not produced before. His great abilities, and his connection with the Sanscrit College and the Education Department, gave Vidyasagar immense influence and power, and he exerted that influence to reward real merit. He appreciated the talent and genius of Akshay Kumar, and when the post of Deputy Inspectors of schools was created, Vidyasagar offered one of them, with a pay Rs. 150 a month, to Akshay Kumar. The latter was then getting only Rs. 60 a month as editor of *Tatvabodhini*, but his duty impelled him to the task and Akshay Kumar had no higher pleasure in life than performance of his duty. He therefore declined without a pang the more lucrative appointment offered to him.

But the philanthropic Vidyasagar would not be thwarted.

When the Normal School was established in Calcutta, Vidyasagar settled with the authorities that Akshay Kumar would be its head teacher on a pay of Rs. 200 a month. Akshay Kumar wished to decline this offer also, and it was only at Vidyasagar's strong and presistent request that he was compelled to accept it. The annals of literature are replete with stories of mutual jealousies between rival authors; it is with sincere gratification, therefore, that we record this evidence of cordial good feelings between Vidyasagar and Akshay Kumar,—feelings which reflect equal honour on both the great writers.

It was in 1855, that he withdrew himself from the work in connection with the *Patrika,* and became Head teacher of the Calcutta Normal School. But his disease became worse, and he had to resign the appointment after two or three years. The year which marked the death of Isvar Chandra Gupta witnessed the practical retirement of Akshay Kumar from all work.

He lived for nearly thirty years in enforced privacy and retirement. One great work issued from his retirement; it is an account of the Hindu sects, adapted from H. H. Wilson's English work, and prefaced by a long dissertation on the Hindu Aryans which is a masterpiece of learning and erudition, conveyed in forcible and graceful style.

After nearly thirty years of an inactive life, the talented Akshay Kumar passed away from us in 1886. He lived to see the fruits of his labour; and the generation which had grown up around him in his closing days had been educated on his works, imbued with that healthy knowledge which he laboured to spread, and with that earnest spirit of progress which he endeavoured to infuse. He lived also to see the Bengali style, which he and Vidyasagar had dignified, made richer day by day by varied and meritorious works.

The great merit of Akshay Kumar's style is its earnestness, its surpassing vigour and force. We quote a few pasages below,[2] and the reader will be able to judge for himself. The

[2] kichukāl itastataḥ bhramaṇ ānantar dūr haite ek apūrva sarovar dekhite pāilām evaṁ taddarśanārthe āmār atyanta kautūhal upasthit haila| krame krame nikaṭvartī haiyā dekhi, katakguli parampavitra sarvāṅgasundarī kanyā sarovartale vicaraṇ karitechen/tāṁhāder asāmānya rūp-

style is the man, and Akshay Kumar's style reflects the true patriot and the earnest, enthusiastic reformer. Vidyasagar's style appears to us to be more finished and refined, Akshay Kumar's is more forcible and earnest. In Vidyasagar's style we admire the placid stillness and soft beauty of a quiet lake, reflecting on its bosom the gorgeous tints of the sky and the surrounding objects. In Akshay Kumar's style we admire the vehemence and force of the mountain torrent in its wild and rugged beauty. Vidyasagar is the more accomplished master of style, Akshay Kumar is the more forcible preacher. Modern Bengali prose, as we understand it, has been shaped by these twin workers whose memory will be long preserved in Bengal.

We have said before that both these writers were enthusiastic in the cause of social reform. Vidyasagar's great work of reform was to ameliorate the condition of Hindu widows, and to legalize their remarriage. Akshay Kumar was compelled by his illness to retire early from the field of active work, and could not take a part in this noble movement; but the last extract which we have quoted below shews

lāvaṇya, praphulla pavitra mukhaśrī evaṁ sāralya o vātsalya svabhāv avalokan kariyā aparimeya prīti lābh karilām/āścarya ei ye, tāṁhādiger śarīre kona alaṇkār nāi, athaca analaṇkāri tāṁhāder alaṅkār haiyāche|

* * * *

vidyā devir upadeśanusāre āmi ullikhita śānti-sāgare avagāhan kariyā abhūtapūrva ati nirmal ānanda-nīre nimagna haitechilām, itimadhye nidrābhaṅga haiyā dekhi, sei sundar mārut-sevita yamunā-kūlei śayita haiyā rahiyāchi| — [Cārupāṭh, III—vidyā-viṣayak svapna darśan]

mahāval parākrānta vīryavanta pūrva-puruṣerā ek haste hala-yantra o apar haste raṇa-śastra grahaṇ pūrvak, putra-kalatra-dauhitrādir agraṇī haiyā, utsāhita aśaṅkita mane, sneha-pālita godhan saṅge, bhāratvarṣa praveś karitechen, iha smaraṇ o cintā karā, ki aparisīm ānanderi viṣay ?

* * * *

[*Bhārat-varṣīya upāsak sampradāy*,
I, Āryagaṇer bhāratvarṣa preveś|]

yāṁhāder duḥkha dekhiyā dayār udrek hay nā pātak dekhiyā aśraddhār ābirbhāv hay nā, e viṣaye tāṁhāder parāmarśa jijñāsā karibār prayojan nāi|

* * * *

yini kona nava vidhavā taruṇī strīke sadyomṛta priya patir śoka-mohe muhyamānā, dharātale luṇṭhamānā o aharniś rorudyamānā darśan kariyā kātar haiyāchen, tāṁhākei jijñāsā kari, "vidhavā-vivāha pracalita haoyā ucit kinā ? —(*Vidhavā Vivāha*)

* * * *

how earnestly, how intensely he felt on the subject. Every true-hearted Hindu must feel keenly on the subject; but it is given only to men like Akshay Kumar and Vidyasagar, who combine a manly courage with true tenderness of heart, to battle against unreasoning prejudices and heartless selfishness in the cause of reform.

It would be going somewhat beyond the scope of our work to indicate the influence which Akshay Kumar exerted on the Brahmo Samaj to which he belonged. His biographer, Pandit Mahendra Nath informs us, that it was Akshay Kumar's uncompromising regard for truth which led him to question the infallibility of the *Vedanta*. He thought on the subject, and discussed it with his fellow-workers, until the Brahmo community were at last persuaded to reject the doctrine of the infallibility of the ancient scriptures, while they still continued to revere them as holy and venerable works, nobly fitted for our instruction and guidance. This was one of the most noted changes in the history of the Brahmo Samaj, and it was due to Akshay Kumar, more than to any one else.

We are indebted also to Pandit Mahendra Nath Vidyanidhi for many passages from the writings and speeches of Akshay Kumar, which have never yet been published in a collected form, but which are instinct with eloquence and beauty. A complete edition of Akshay Kumar's literary works has yet to be published, and we look to the Brahmo Samaj for the performance of this patriotic task.

OTHER RELIGIOUS WRITERS

A host of talented writers continued the work when Akshay Kumar retired from the field. The venerable Debendra Nath Tagore continued to preside over the Brahmo Samaj, and issued a series of religious works which have greatly benefited and dignified Bengali prose. Raj Narayan Basu, the companion and collaborator of Akshay Kumar, has enriched the language by a series of lectures and discourses mostly on religious subjects. The sons of Debendra Nath have distinguished themselves in literature and song, and the Bengali language will bear on it the impress of the work of this talented and cultured family. Keshab Chandra Sen and his section of the Brahmo Samaj have followed in the footsteps of Debendra Nath, and have enriched Bengali lierature by sermons and lectures. And Pandit Siva Nath Sastri, who heads the third section of the Samaj, is also the writer of meritorious works. Thus modern Bengali literature owes much to the religious movement initiated by Ram Mohan Roy.

CHAPTER XVI

Isvar Chandra Vidyasagar

(*1820-1891*)

Akshay Kumar and Isvar Chandra were twin workers in the field of social reform and literary culture. Isvar Chandra began a little later than Akshay Kumar, but his endeavours were more arduous and more prolonged, and the scene of his struggles against social abuses lay not only in the arena of letters, but also in the arena of actual life.

Isvar Chandra was born in 1820 in the village of Birsinha, which was within the limits of Hooghly District at one time. but is now within the limits of Midnapur. He was the eldest son of his father Thakurdas Banerjea, who held a humble post in Calcutta on Rs. 10 a month. Like Akshay Kumar, he received his early training in his village Pathshala, but was removed by his father to Calcutta at the age of nine, and was admitted in the Sanscrit College. Isvar Chandra suffered all the privations of poverty; he lodged in poor quarters, lived on poor food, cooked his own meals, and wore ragged clothes, while he was prosecuting his studies. And not unoften he suffered from the pangs of hunger, and went without a meal. Few of the thousands of students who prosecute their studies in our schools in the present day have any idea of the privations which poor Isvar had to go through, sixty years ago.

In the midst of such privations, young Isvar Chandra distinguished himself by his remarkable intelligence, and generally held the first place in his class. He studied Sanscrit Grammar, Literature, Astronomy, Sacred Law, and Philosophy, distinguished himself by his compositions in Sanscrit prose and verse, and also picked up a slight knowledge of English. In 1839 he finished his education by passing an examination in Hindu Law, and obtained the title of Vidyasagar; and in 1841 he was appointed Head Pandit of Fort William College, on a pay of Rs. 50. It was then that young Vidyasagar began to improve his knowledge of English.

Five years later, when Akshay Kumar was swaying the ideas and opinions of thoughtful and earnest men in Bengal by his articles in the *Tatvabodhini Patrka,* Iswar Chandra was appointed Assistant Secretary to the Sanscrit College. The following year, 1847, witnessed the publication of his first literary work, *Betal-Panchabinsati.* The work marked an epoch in the history of Begali prose, and the beauty and richness of Vidyasagar's style disclosed resources of the Bengali language which no one had suspected before. Nevertheless, like all first attempts, *Betal* had its faults; the style was too ornate, and a little to artificial.

Isvar Chandra was a man of great independence of character. His suggestions in some matters were not accepted by Rasamay Dutt,[1] then Secretary to the Sanscrit College and a leading man of his time, and Isvar Chandra resigned his appointment as Assistant Secretary.

He entered the Fort William College once more as a Head Clerk, and soon associated himself with the great and good-hearted Drinkwater Bethune in the cause of female education in Bengal. And in 1850 the management of girls' school, called after Bethune, was entrusted entirely to the enthusiastic Pandit. In the same year he re-entered the Sanscrit College as Professor of literature, in the post vacated by Madan Mohan Tarkalankar, of whom we have spoken before. But a higher honour was in store for him. Rasamay Dutt resigned his post about this time, the posts of Secretary and Assistant Secretary were amalgamated into that of Principal, and Isvar Chandra Vidyasagar was appointed the first Principal of the Sanscrit College.

Vidyasagar had now ample opportunities to reform the method of teaching in that institution, and his modern and easy method is appreciated by thousands of young Bengali who have studied Sanscrit Since. It became possible, under this method, to 'acquire a knowledge of Sanscrit without shutting one-self out from all other learning and knowledge in the universe.

[1] The proper spelling is Datta. But we write the name as it is written by the members of this cultured family.

Educational work of all kinds crowded on Vidyasagar thick and fast. His friend Bethune died in 1851, and the Lieutenant Governor, Sir Frederick Halliday, placed in Bethune School under the management of Vidyasagar. The great scheme of establishing aided schools all over Bengal was inaugurated in 1854, and Vidyasagar submitted his masterly report for carrying out that scheme. His plan was approved, and he was appointed Inspecter of Hooghly, Burdwan, Midnapur and Nadia on a pay of Rs. 200, in addition to Rs. 300 which he was now getting as Pricipal of Sanscrit College. He organized boys' schools in the four districts, established over 40 girls' schools in Hooghly and Burdwan, and superintended the work of the Sanscrit College and the Normal school in Calcutta. In the midst of these vast labours he never rested from his literary work; his *Sakuntala*, adapted from the Sanscrit drama of Kalidas, was published in 1855.

But a task, mightier than educational reform and literary culture, now attracted the attention and the energies of the great and manly worker. Great as was his intellect, Vidyasagar's heart was yet greater, and the unfortunate condition of his countrywomen often affected him to tears. The wrongs of Hindu widows aroused his strongest sympathy, and he now prepared himself for a great movement to redress those wrongs.

It did not take a Pandit of Vidyasagar's learning much time to discover that the ancient Hindu scriptures did not enjoin perpetual widowhood; and in 1855 he startled the Hindu world by his work on the remarriage of Hindu widows. The excitement which the work, coming from the pen of a learned Brahman, caused among the orthodox Hindus of the day cannot be described. Abuse and vituperation were poured forth from all sides on his devoted head, pamphlets and publications purporting to point out his mistake were issued in quick succession, songs were composed and sung in Calcutta and in remote districts, rediculing Vidyasagar and his great endeavour. Amidst this storm of indignation which he had raised, Vidyasagar stood unappalled and unmoved. He issued a second book on the subject, replying to all the arguments which had been brought against his position, and replying to them with a wealth of learning and a facility of expression which silenced opposition, and practically closed the controversy! Not content with this literary triumph, Vidyasagar associated himself with all the influential men of his time, with Prasanna Kumar Tagore, Ram Gopal Ghosh, Pratap Chandra Sinha and others, and appealed to the Government to declare that the sons of remarried Hindu widows should be considered legitimate heirs. The Government of the day responded to this reasonable demand against unreasoning opposition and heartless selfishness, and the measure was passed into law in 1856.

But the reformer's work was only half done. Vidyasagar was not the man to sleep in the shade of his laurels. He raised subscriptions in the cause of widow-marriages, and the very year, in which the law was passed, witnessed the celebration of the marriage of a Hindu widow with Srish Chandra Vidyasagar, then Judge-Pandit of Murshidabad. Other intances followed, and some years later the indomitable reformer gave his only son in marriage with a widow. Never since the days of Ram Mohan Roy had Bengal witnessed such single-hearted devotion in the cause of reform, such triumph of humanity over the wrongs and abuses of centuries. Widow-marriages have not been very frequent in Hindu society since that time, but the path is now open; and Hindu fathers who will have the courage to save their girls of tender years from life-long widowhood will bless the name of the great reformer for generations to come.

Vidyasagar did not long retain his appointment under the Government. His great independence of character did not always please his superiors, and he resigned his appointments, worth Rs. 500 a month, in 1858. Four years after he produced his master work, *Sitar Banabas,* based on Bhavabhuti's finest drama in Sanscrit. Whether we consider the grace and elegance of the style, the skilfulness of the narration, or the tenderness and pathos which pervade the work, we must rank it among the noblest production in Bengali prose.

Minor works proceeded from the pen of the veteran writer in quick succession, and were welcomed and adopted in schools all over Bengal. The Princely income which Vidyasagar thus derived was devoted to the relief of suffering and distress. Hundreds of widows and orphans owed their living and education to his charity, every great cause, every worthy movement, received his support, and the greatest and richest zemindars of the land delighted to honour the venerable Pandit who lived a simple life, whose courage in the cause of reform was indomitable, whose kindness and charity were inexhaustible. The name of Vidyasagar became a household word all over Bengal, his charities were far-reaching and extensive, his help was sought for by those in distress and never sought in vain, and his books were read by the young and the old. Vidyasagar was scarcely better known as an author than as a reformer and a philanthropist.

One more lofty aim attracted his attention in his later days. The system of polygamy, specially prevalent among the Kulin classes of Bengal, is degrading to men, and causes untold suffering to women, and the veteran reformer grided up his loins once more in the cause of reform. He published works proving that the ancient Hindu Sastras do not sanction polygamy without restriction, and are not as merciless to women as modern Hindu castom has come to be. Once more, orthodox Hindu society felt the blow from the gauntleted hand of the Pandit. Replies were attempted, and abuse was showered on the reformer in vain, for Vidyasagar stood unmoved. It was not possible however for the Government to prohibit polygamy by law, and the triumph of Vidyasagar in this instance remained only a literary triumph.

This was Vidyasagar's last great endeavour. The last fifteen years of his life were spent in well-earned repose, and the Governmnt created him a Companion of the Indian Empire in 1877. His zeal for progress remained unabated, and he never hesitated to extend a helping hand to those who needed his help.[2] His charities too continued unabated, and thus passed the closing years of the great author, reformer and philanthropist, until he died in 1891, lamented all over Bengal as no man has ever been lamented within our recollection. Monuments of marble and bronze lie scattered all over our

[2] My readers will pardon my citing a characteristic instance which concerns myself. When I commenced a translation of the Rigveda Sanhita into the vernacular of Bengal in 1885, my endeavour to popularize the ancient scriptures met with a perfect storm of opposition from my orthodox countrymen. Among the few Pandits who encouraged me in the task was the venerable Isvar Chandra Vidyasagar.

metropolis in memory of men considered great, because they held high posts in their day. The monument of Vidyasagar is in the hearts of his countrymen, and will remain for ever enshrined in their grateful recollections.[3]

OTHER PROSE WRITERS

At the close of an account of Vidyasagar's life, some mention should be made of Bhudeb Mukherji, who succeeded Vidyasagar as an educationist, and has also written some works in Bengali prose. He was born in Calcutta, and was junior to Vidyasagar by five years; and he was educated first in the Sanscrit College, and then in the Hindu College. After filling the posts of Head Master of Howrah School and Superintendent of Hooghly Normal School, Bhudeb became Assistant Inspector of Schools in 1862, and eventually Inspector of a Division in 1869. He was made a Companion of the Indian Empire in 1877, and member of the Bengal Council in 1882, and in the following year he retired from service. He died in 1894. His earliest works are two historical tales in Bengali, adapted from a well known English book called Romance of History. His latest works are his three thoughtful *Prabandhas* or essays on domestic life, society, and ceremonial rites, which fill nearly eight hundred pages of his printed works.

Another historical romance is *Bangadhip Parajaya* by Pratap Chandra Ghosh. Hara Chandra Ghosh succeeded Rasamay Dutt as Judge of the Court of Small Causes in Calcutta. Both were leading men in their time, and they were the first Bengalees who filled that high and responsible post. Pratap Chandra is the son of Hara Chandra Ghosh, and his work is connected with the story of the conquest of Raja Pratapaditya of Jessore, by Man Sinha the general of Akbar.

A more witty writer was Pyari Chand Mitra, and his *Alaler-gharer Dulal* is a social tale of Bengal. It has been translated into English.

The patriotic zemindar Kali Prasanna Sinha also wrote a satirical sketch on modern society called *Hutam Pechar Naksha;* but he has done more lasting service to the cause of Bengali literature and modern progress by his meritorious translation of the Sanscrit *Mahabharata* into Bengali prose.

The work had been translated into Bengali by the Pandits of the Maharaja of Burdwan some years before, but Kali Prasanna Sinha's translation is simpler and more literal, and is more acceptable to the public. He employed a number of Pandits to make this translation, and widely distributed the work, free of cost, among those who took an interest in the ancient epic.

The example of Kali Prasanna Sinha was not lost, and the *Ramayana* was published in original Sanscrit, with a meritorious prose translation into Bengali, by Pandit Hem Chandra Vidyaratna in 1868 to 1885.

Kali Prasanna Sinha's *Mahabharata* and Hem Chandra Vidyaratna's *Ramayana* are the best prose translations of those epics in the Bengali language.

[3] The following is a fair specimen of Vidyāsagar's style :—

lakṣmaṇke eirūp śokābhibhūta dekhiyā sitā kahilen, vatsa tomār aparādh ki ? tumi kena akāraṇe eta kātar haitecha o paritāp karitecha ? tomār upar ruṣṭa vā asantuṣṭa haivār kathā dūre thākuk, āmi kāyamanovākye devatādiger nikaṭ niyata ei prārthanā kariva, yena janmāntare tomāri mata guṇer devar pāi ; tumi cirajīvî hao|

* * * *

ei valiyā, snehabhare vāraṁvār āśīrvād kariyā, sitā lakṣmaṇke prasthān karite valilen|

* * * *

takhan lakṣmaṇ ār sītāke lakṣita karite nā pāriyā hāhākār o śire karāghāt kariyā rodan karite lāgilen| sītār rath nayan-pather atit haivāmātra yūtha-virahita kurarīr nyāy uccaiḥsvare krandan karite ārambha karilen.

A more eloquent passage on the cruel custom of enforced widowhood is quoted below :—

hā bharātvarṣa ! tumi ki hatabhāgya ! tumi tomār pūrvatana santānganer ācār-guṇe puṇyabhūmi valiyā sarvatra paricita haiyāchile, kintu tomār idānīntan santānerā — tomāke yerūp puṇyabhūmi kariyā tuliyāchen, tāhā bhāviyā dekhile sarva-śarīre śoṇit śuṣka haiyā yāy|

* * * *

hāy ki paritāper viṣay ! ye deśer puruṣ-jātir dayā nāi, dharma nāi, nyāy anyāy vicār nāi, hitāhit bodh nāi, sadvivecanā nāi, keval laukik rakṣāi pradhān karma o param dharma. ār yena se deśe hatabhāgya avalājāti janmagrahaṇ nā kare|

CHAPTER XVII

DRAMATIC WRITERS: DINA BANDHU MITRA
(1829-1873)

KULINA-KULA-SARVASVA is said to be the first original dramatic work in Bengali. It was composed in 1854, and indicates the spirit of the times. The veteran satirist, Isvar Chandra Gupta, was still hurling his sarcasms on all social reforms, but the shafts of his wit fell piontless among the earnest workers of the day. The Hindu College was yielding its annual crop of young men with English education and western notions: Akshay Kumar had educated his countrymen in advanced ideas; and the great Vidyasagar had espoused the cause of female education, and was even then meditating his memorable attack on the cruel custom of enforced widowhood. It was at such a time, in 1854, that the first original dramatic composition, *Kulina-Kula-Sarvasva* held up the custom of Kulinism and polygamy to deserved ridicule and contempt.

The author, Ram Narayan Tarkaratna, was junior to Vidyasagar by three years, being born in 1823; and was educated in the Sanscrit College. He then became a teacher in the College, retird on pension in his old age, and died in 1885.

The history of the stage in Bengal deserves a brief narration. *Jatra* and other theatrical performances of the old style were the pastime of our fathers, and *Kabi, Pachali* and *Half-Akrai* were then in fashion. But the *Sans-Souci* theatre was established in Chowringhee early in the century, and men like H. H. Wilson, the oriental scholar, and Hume, Magistrate of Calcutta, took part in the performances. Indian gentlemen witnessed these performances, and occasionally got up theatrical performances among themselves; and Shakespeare's plays were acted in English, or Sanscrit dramas were acted in Bengali translations. At the special request of Jotindra Mohan Tagore, (now Maharaja Sir Jotindra Mohan Tagore,) Ram Narayan's original drama *Kulina-Kula-Sarvasva* was acted in 1856 in the premises of the Oriental Seminary. In the following year the eminent Kali Prasanna

Sinha, translator of the Mahabharata, had his own translation of *Vikramorvasi* acted in his house with great pomp and magnificence, the translator himself taking a part on the stage. The performance excited a great deal of interest in the town.

It was then decided between Jotindra Mohan Tagore and Rajas Pratap Chandra and Isvar Chandra of the Paikpara Raj family to get up a permanent theatrical house on a grand scale for the encouragement of the Bengali drama. The scheme was matured, and Ram Narayan the author of *Kulina-Kula-Sarvasva* was to compose a new drama. The magnificent garden house of Belgachia, belonging to the Paikpara Rajas, was to be the scene of the new theatre. No expense would be spared to make the scenic decoration and the performance a success.

It was under such auspices that Pandit Ram Narayan's second drama, *Ratnavali,* was to be acted. But the Rajas had many friends among the European officials of Calcutta, and they desired to witness the performance. It was necessary to invite them; it was necessary to make an English translation of the drama in order to enable them to follow the acting.

This was the first introduction of the greatest literary genius of the century into the arena of letters. Madhu Sudan Datta was a brilliant student of the Hindu College. He had become a Christian and had gone to Madras, where he had worked as a teacher, and distinguished himself by his "Captive Ladie" and other compositions in English verse. He had now returned to Calcutta and held an appointment in the Police Court. He was selected to translate the new drama for the English visitors, and he did it with credit and distinction.

At last in July 1958, the drama was acted under circumstances of pomp and scenic decorations which surpassed the utmost expectations. The Lieutenant-Governor of Bengal, the Judges of the High Court, and other high officials witnessed the performance. Every one was charmed with the acting; a new era was opened for the Bengal Drama.

Madhu Sudan's ambition was fired. He had written much in English verse, and had written with ability and poetic talent, but all attempts to court the Muses in a foreign tongue must be fruitless. His genius saw at a glance its true scope. Madhu Sudan who had hitherto never written a line of Bengali prose or verse, Madhu Sudan who almost despised the Bengali language,—was impelled by his "vaulting ambition" to be a Bengali author! His friends laughed at the idea; they did not know what is possible for true genius to attempt, and to achieve.

Madhu Sudan was thus the first student of the Hindu College, properly educated in English, who turned to Bengali literature. All the renowned authors who had hitherto served their mother-tongue, Isvar Chandra Gupta, Akshay Kumar Datta, Isvar Chandra Vidyasagar and others, were men who had acquired an imperfect knowledge of English, mostly by their own endeavours. The *alumnii* of the Hindu College had hitherto looked with contempt on Bengali literature, had written prose and verse in English, had hoped to distinguish themselves in English literature. The truth came like a flash of inspiration to Madhu Sudan Datta that true genius mistakes its vocation when it struggles in a foreign tongue. Madhu Sudan lived to correct his mistake and to be the most eminent poet in his own language. And since Madhu Sudan's time the *alumnii* of our schools and Colleges,—those who have sought literary fame and were worthy of it,—have won their laurels in their mother tongue.

The success of *Ratnavali* inspired Madhu Sudan with the idea of writing a Bengali drama. He went to the Asiatic Society's rooms, took away some Sanscrit dramas and Bengali works, read them, and pondered on them. He then put his hand to the task he had imposed on himself, and his genius carried him through. The result was *Sarmishtha,* one of the best and most beautiful plays in Bengali. The production was submitted to Prem Chand Tarkavagish a learned Pandit of the day, but Prem Chand returned it with the remark that it had sinned against all the rules of the Sanscrit drama!' Madhu Sudan was then advised to accept the suggestions of Ram Narayan the successful author of *Ratnavali;* but he would have none of it, and only adopted some of his verbal corrections. He truly wrote to a friend on this occasion,— "You know that a man's style is the reflection of his mind, and I am afraid there is little congeniality between our friend and my poor self. However, I shall adopt some of his corrections."[1]

The drama was acted at Belgachia theatre with great success, Jotindra Mohan Tagore himself composing some songs for the piece.

Both Ram Narayan and Madhu Sudan lived to compose some more dramas, Ram Narayan's *Naba Natak* is a clever hit on his countrymen who seek to indulge in the joys of wedded life a an advanced age, and marry girl-wives. Madhu Sudan's *Padmavati* and *Krishna Kumari* are meritorious works, the latter being based on the story of the princess of Udaypur whose tragic fate threw a gloom over Rajasthan early in this century. Madhu Sudan then turned to blank verse and to epic poetry; and the story of his success in that line and of his life will be told in another chapter.

As Madhu Sudan retired from the field of Bengali drama, his place was filled by a writer who has won a higher dintinction in this department of literature. The new writer was Dina Bandhu Mitra. All the first three dramatists of Bengal were of nearly the same age; Ram Narayan was born in 1823, Madhu Sudan in 1824, and Dina Bandhu in 1829. Like Madhu Sudan Datta, Dina Bandhu was educated in the Hindu College; he distinguished himself in government service in the postal department; but he devoted his talents to the improvement of his mother tongue. He died in 1873.

The oppression of the Indigo Planters of Nadia and Jessore was the subject of complaint for many years; and our readers will fiind an extract which we have given from Isvar Chandra Gupta's poetry in which the poet has indulged in a feeling appeal to the Queen of England against this oppression. The oppression however continued unchecked, and Dina Bandhu. who was born in Chauberia village in Nadia District, had ample opportunities to note the doings of the planters and their subordinates. At last in 1860, he published his first dramatic work, *Nil Darpan,* anonymously, bringing together facts and incidents which had come under his observation, and weaving them into the main plot with skill of a true artist.

The literary beauties of the work are by no means insigni-

[1] See Jogendra Nath Basu's life of Michael Madhu Sudan Datta.

ficant. An honest family and its most amiable inmates enlist the sympathy of the reader from the beginning, and at last wake in him the keenest sorrow for their misfortunes. All the members of the family are well delineated. The old, simple-minded, affectionate father, the elder son managing the estate and the younger studying at a College in Calcutta, and their wives, the most innocent amiable creatures in the world, have all been well delineated. Clouds gather on the horizon of their felicity and thicken as the story proceeds, and there are few readers who can read to the end without feeling deeply affected.

The sensation caused by the drama was great. The Rev. J. Long, a true-hearted missionary and friend of the people, translated the work into English in order to hold up to the powers that be, a picture of the oppression which was going on under the British rule, for the pecuniary benefit of British adventurers and speculators. This was too much for the European residents of Calcutta, and their organ the *Englishman.* A prosecution was instituted against the Rev. James Long, and he was thus immortalized. The memory of the benevolent missionary, who was fined and imprisoned in the case, is still cherished by the people of Bengal for what he did, and what he suffered for them.

High-handed exercise of power does not always prepetuate a wrong, and the wrong suffered by the raiyats of Bengal from the indigo planters was too glaring to be bolstered up by an unjust prosecution. The Indigo Commission published a report and made disclosures which could not be gainsaid, and Sir John Peter Grant, the Lieutenant Governor of Bengal, did his best to befriend the raiyats. But the deliverance of the raiyats came from themselves, they combined, all over Nadia, nor to grow indigo, and they submitted to every outrage rather than yield to the planters. Factory after factory failed in consequence of this combination, and the oppression of indigo planters is a thing of the past in the Nadia District.

Nothing afterwards written by Dina Bandhu can compare with *Nila Darpan* from a literary point of view. In his *Nabin-Tapasvini* and *Lilavati* there are undoubtedly fine passages, but still there is nothing to equal the pathos which pervades the *Nil Darpan.* In fact the most popular and the best known of Dina Bandhu's later productions like *Sadhabar Ekadasi* and *Jamai Barik* are popular and successful farces, and Dina Bandhu is known to his countrymen more as a humourist and stirist than as a serious dramatic writer. But there is a difference between Dina Bandhu's satires and Isvar Chandra's satires. Isvar Chandra is opposed to all social progress, and he pours forth his withering scorn in his own matchless verse on new-fangled ways. Dina Bandhu is not opposed to any section, he is too good-natured and good-hearted to attack any particular community, he only ridicules folly and vice. The lash of Isvar Chandra's satire cuts deep, Dina Bandhu's milder and gentler admonitions inflict no wound, but hold up vice only in its natural and hedious colours. Isvar Chandra is the more powerful satirist, Dina Bandhu is the pleasanter humourist. Isvar Chandra's ready and witty verse was the war cry of his party, and the barbed and pointed shafts of his vigorous if coarse sarcasms were the weapons of their war. Dina Bandhu waged no party-strife; his good-natured humour spread a sunshine of gladness around him, and his ridicule of vice and folly was appreciated by all.

Dina Bandhu also wrote some poems, which are distinguished by a harmonious flow of verse. One instance will suffice.[3]

[2] *surapur samapur śāntipur dhām,*
gāy gāy aṭṭālikā śobhā abhirām,
kivā ghāṭ, kivā rāṭ, kivā phulavan,
ye dike cāhiye dekhi juḍāy nayan |
* * * *
śāntipure ḍure sāḍī saramer ari,
"nilāmbarī", "ulaṅginī" "sarvāṅgasundarī" |
sāri sāri kata nārī navīnā sundarī,
caliteche hāsyamukhe path ālo kari,
rājiche mohan mal cañcal caraṇe,
uḍiche añcal cāru cala samīraṇe,
* * * *
guptipāḍā gaṇḍagrām viparit pāre,
kulīn bāmun kata kevalite pāre |
gaurave kulīngaṇ vale dambha kare,
"ṣāṭ vatsarer meye āibuḍa ghare" |
* * * *
ek ek kulīner śata śata viye,
rākhiyāche nām dhām khātāy likhiye |

—*Suradhunī Kāvya*

The Bengali Stage

Dina Bandhu lived to see the Bengali stage based on a permanent basis,—the patronage of the play-going public. The Bengal Theatre was started shortly before the death of the dramatist, and it has been succeeded by a number of theatrical houses, some of which leave little to be desired in orderly management, scenic decorations, and meritorious acting. The institution, which the Rajas of Paikpara wished to create and to foster in 1856 and in subsequent years from their own resources, became a permanent institution of the land before twenty years had passed; and it now looks up, not to Rajas and chiefs, but to an enlightened public for support. The *Kabi*, the *Pachali*, the *Half-Akrai* are things of the past; *Jatras* too do not attract crowds in the metropolis as they did before; the educated public prefer to see modern dramas put on the stage with all the latest improvements and scenic decorations.

Among the successors of Dina Bandhu Mitra, whose name is legion, it will be enough to mention a few of the best. Mano Mohan Basu is the Nestor among the living dramatists, and his *Sati Natak, Harish Chandra, Ramabhisek,* and other plays will always be read with interest and profit. Jyotirindra Nath Tagore has written *Asrumati* and various other plays, and the talented Rabindranath has composed *Raja o Rani* among other works. And lastly, Raj Krishna Roy has composed *Prahlad Charitra* and some other popular plays, but is better known as the translator of *Ramayana* into Bengali verse. Some of our actors on the stage are also the writers of clever plays and meritorious farces.

But a really great dramatic genius has yet to rise in Bengal. The drama has not kept pace in merit with poetry and fiction, of which we will speak in the next two chapters.

CHAPTER XVIII

Madhu Sudan Datta and his Epic Poetry
(1824-1873)

Madhu Sudan Datta is the greatest literary genius of this century, and the full record of his life, compiled by Jogendra Chandra Basu, is the most meritorious biographical work yet written in the Bengali language. This work will be our guide in the present chapter.

Madhu Sudan was born in 1824 in the village of Sagandari in the District of Jessore. His father Raj Narayan Datta had four wives, Madhu Sudan being the child of the eldest. Raj Narayan was a man of property and substance, and a pleader of the Sadar Dewani Adalat. Madhu Sudan remained with him in Calcutta, and was admitted in the Hindu College at the age of thirteen.

The Hindu College, which was established in 1817, effected a revolution in the ideas of the young Hindus of the day. They imbibed in that College a warm appreciation of western literature and western civilization, and brooked with impatience the unreasoning restrictions which modern Hindu customs had imposed on them. Trained under teachers like Derozio and D. L. Richardson, the first young men who came out from the Hindu College were fired with an ambition to reform all that was unhealthy, and to reject all that was hartful, in Hindu customs and rules. The reaction against the restrictions of ages went perhaps a little too far, but we can scarcely regret this reaction to which is really due all the steady improvement and reform which have been effected in this century. One may laugh at the anglicised young collegiates of the first half of this century, but it was those young collegiates whose advanced ideas and training leavened the society in which they lived, and made the sober reforms of later times possible. Men like Kashi Prasad Ghosh, Ram Gopal Ghosh and Rama Prasad Roy, like K. M. Banerjea, Debendra Nath Tagore and Prasanna Kumar Tagore, were among the early students of the Hindu College, and the ideas which they received with their English education permeated the society in which they lived. The writings of Akshay Kumar Datta reflected the progress infused into Hindu society through the Hindu College. The reforms effected by Isvar Chandra Vidyasagar were possible only after Hindu society had been permeated with advanced ideas through a healthy English education. For a time the *alumnii* of the Hindu College stood aloof from directly taking a part in improving their national literature; they stiil indulged in dreams of distinguishing themselves in English. But the dream was dispelled in time, and when the ardent young collegemen espoused the cause of their own national literature, they achieved results which silenced their critics and astonished their best friends. The present century has produced nothing in verse comparable to that of Madhu Sudan and nothing in prose comparable to that of Bankim Chandra.

Madhu Sudan remained in the Hindu College for six years, from 1837 to 1842, and distinguished himself among a band of young men who were remarkably intelligent. Pyari Charan Sarkar, Prasanna Kumar Sarbadhikari, Gobind Chandra Dutt, Shashi Chandra Dutt, Jagadish Nath Roy, Kishori Chand Mitra, Ganendra Mohan Tagore, Bhudeb Mukherji, Raj Narayan Basu, and Bhola Nath Chandra were students of the Hindu College at the same time with Madhu Sudan; and one of his fellow students writes that Madhu Sudan was the Jupiter among these stars of the Hindu College.

Like many young students of the Hindu College, Madhu Sudan began to write English verse, some of which has been preserved by his biographer. Love and misanthrophy were the favourite themes in those times when Byron's poetry still held the world in thrall, but some patriotic poems, like that on king Porus, indicate that Madhu Sudan felt for his country like the other young men of his day. Permeated with western ideas, the young poet longed to visit Europe even in those early days, and was filled with an ambition for glory or a nameless grave in Albion's distant shore.

It was during his college days that Madhu Sudan's father desired to give the young man in marriage, and a suitable bride was selected. Madhu Sudan objected, but his father insisted on the marriage. This was the turning point in Madhu Sudan's life. He ran away to Christian missionaries, was concealed for four days in Fort William, and in February, 1843, was baptised and took the name of Michael Madhu Sudan.

This incident is only one more illustration of the maxim that senseless coercion leads to violent reaction. Madhu Sudan's father and mother were no doubt worthy people; but young Madhu Sudan must have contemplated with grief and humiliation the domestic arrangement under which his mother shared her husband's affection with three other fellow-wives. And when his father determined to marry him against his wishes and entreaties, the young man took the first step which offered itself to him to escape, and became a Christian. The history of social reforms in the present century illustrates the truth that great absues lead to reform, senseless coercion leads to reaction.

Madhu Sudan now studied in the Bishop's College for four years, his fond father still paying the expenses of his education. Madhu Sudan had learned English and Persian in the Hindu College; he now learned Greek, Latin and Sanscrit in the Bishop's College. Later in life he studied and learnt Telegu and Tamil in Madras, he picked up French, German and Italian in Europe, and he had also some knowledge of Hebrew. Madhu Sudan was thus one of the most distinguished linguists among our countrymen.

The relations between Madhu Sudan and his father gradually became strained, and Madhu Sudan felt himself lonely and without a friend in the world. Some Madras students attended the Bishop's College, and Madhu Sudan secretly resolved to leave his province and to try his chances at Madras. He secretly completed all arrangements, and in 1848, sailed for Madras.

His first days in Madras were days of poverty, wretchedness and distress. Poverty impelled him to write to the local papers, and his elegant composition soon attracted attention. He once more launched into compositions in English verse, and the story of Prithu Rai, the last Hindu King of Delhi, and his bride Sanjuta, formed the subject of his meritorious poem entitled the *Captive Ladie,* which was published in 1849.

The publication excited the utmost interest in Madras, and an English reviewer wrote in the *Athenæum* that it contained passages which "neither Scott nor Byron would have been ashamed to own." But if Madhu Sudan aspired to win a lasting literary fame by his English poetry, he found out his mistake before long. Even the great and good-hearted Drinkwater Bethune, to whom a copy of the poem was presented, wrote, and wrote truly:

"He could render a far greater service to his country and have a better chance of achieving a lasting reputation for himself if he would employ the taste and talents which he has cultivated by the study of English in improving the standard and adding to the stock of the poems of his own language."

A few days before the publication of his *Captive Ladie,* Madhu Sudan had married the daughter of a European indigo-planter in Madras. Sweet indeed are some of the lines which the poet wrote on his occasion:—

"Yes,—like that star which, on the wilderness
Of vasty ocean, wooes the anxious eye
.Of lonely mariner,—and wooes to bless,—
For there be hope writ on her brow on high :
He recks not darkling waves,—nor fears the lightless sky.
"Oh ! beautiful as inspiration, when
She fills the poet's breast,—her fairy shrine ;—
Wooed by melodious worship ! Welcome then ,—
Though ours the home of want, I ne'er repine, .
Art thou not there, even thou, a priceless gem and mine?"

But the wedded life of the wild and wayward poet was not destined to be thappy. Within a few years after his marriage he was separated from this first wife, and united with the daughter of the Principal of the Madras Presidency College. It was this second wife who stuck to him through life amidst all his weaknesses and misfortunes, and was the mother of the children he has left.

After a stay of eight years in Madras, Madhu Sudan returned to Calcutta in 1856 with his English wife. His ambition to distinguish himself by his English compositions had proved fruitless, and he was as helpless and poor as when he had left Bengal. He accepted the humble post of a clerk, and then of an interpreter, of the Calcutta Police Court. It was in these circumstances of distress that Madhu Sudan first turned to the composition of dramas in his own native language, under circumstances which have been described in the last chapter.

Modhu Sudan's first Bengali work *Sarmishtha* appeared in 1858,—the very year which witnessed the death of his great predecessor, Isvar Chandra Gupta. Madhu Sudan's second drama *Padmavati,* appeared in 1859. The poet followed up his success by two clever farces, unique in his time, one ridiculing the vices and follies of "young Bengal," and the other ridiculing the more dangerous hypocrisy and profligacy of "old Bengal." His successes fired him with a new ambition. He had formed high conceptions of poetry from his deep appreciation of Valmiki and Homer, and he felt within himself a call to imitate the lofty sublimity of those poets. But the jingling of the Bengali rhyme was ill suited to such attempts, and he remarked to his friend and adviser Jotindra Mohan Tagore, that there was no great future for Bengali poetry until the chains of rhyme were rent asunder. Jatindra Mohan replied that blank verse was scarcely suited to the Bengali language, and that even in the French language blank verse was not a success. But, replied Madhu Sudan, Bengali is the daughter of Sanscrit, and nothing is impossible for the child of such a mother! In his enthusiasm Madhu Sudan promised to make the endeavour, and to prove that blank verse in Bengali was possible. Jotindra Mohan listened to the proposal incredulously, but promised to pay for the publication of Madhu Sudan's proposed work, if it was a success. Madhu Sudan set to work with his accustomed impetuosity and zeal, and the *Tilottama*, published in 1860, was the result of this historic conversation.

When this work in blank verse appeared. it took the literary world by surprise. The power of diction, the sublimity of conception, and the beauty of description could not be denied; but nevertheless the reading world wondered at the audacity of the writer and could not believe his work to be a success. Ridicule was hurled on the ambitious writer from all sides, contemptuous parodies were published, and writers of Isvar Chandra Gupta's school, as well of the modern school of Akshay Kumar and Vidyasagar, pronounced the attempt to be a failure! The eminent Vidyasagar himself, ever ready to appreciate and encourage merit, could not pronounce *Tilottama* a success; writers and critics of humbler merit and less candour ridiculed the writer and condemned the work.

Amidst this storm of opposition and ridicule Madhu Sudan stood unmoved. Never was the greatness of his genius, the loftiness of his purpose, the indomitable strength of his will, more manifest. He was resolved to prove by a higher endeavour and a loftier achievement that he was right, and that the world was wrong. It was a repetition of the story of Lord Byron whose earlier poems were condemned, and who retaliated with the might of a giant in his *English Bards* and *Scotch Reviewers.* Only Madhu Sudan retaliated in a nobler manner; he did not abuse his critics, he convinced and silenced them by his success in a higher endeavour.

Among the few who pronounced Madhu Sudan's *Tilottama* to be a success was Jotindra Mohan Tagore himself. He acknowledged the beauty of the work, owned his defeat, and published the work at his own expense. The eminent Rajendralala Mitra, who was issuing the *Bibidhartha Sangraha* from 1851 for spreading culture and general information among his countrymen, was another critic who recognized the success of *Tilottama.* And Raj Narayan Basu, the venerable collaborator of Akshay Kumar Datta, was charmed with the noble performance. "If Indra," he wrote, "had spoken Bengali, he would have spoken in the style of the poem. The author's extraordinary loftiness and brilliancy of imagination, his minute observation of nature, his delicate sense of beauty, the uncommon splendour of his diction, and the rich music of his versification charm us in every page."

But a sceptical world had to be convinced, and the world was convinced by Madhu Sudan's grander poem, *Meghanad-badh*, published in 1861. This time the critics were fairly convinced! The great Vidyasagar admitted his mistake with his accustomed candour, and acknowledged Madhu Sudan's genius and the success of his great endeavour. The voice of ridicule, though not completely silenced, failed to have any effect. All Bengal felt that a new light had dawned on the horizon of the nation's literature, that a genius of the first magnitude had appeared. The munificent Kali Prasanna Sinha, translator of the *Mahabharata,* was one of the strongest admirers of Madhu Sudan, and he convened a meeting of the literary society which he had established to honour the great poet. Rajas Pratap Chandra and Isvar Chandra, the cultured Jotindra Mohan Tagore, the talented Rama Prasad Roy and Digambar Mitra and many others were present on this occasion Madhu Sudan was duly honoured. and the first edition of his Meghanad-Badh was exhausted within one year.

It was in this year, 1861, that Madhu Sudan published his third drama, *Krishna Kumari,* of which we have spoken in the last chapter, as well as his sweet and musical but unfinished work *Brajangana.* And the following year witnessed the publication of the spirited epistles known as the *Birangana.* Within four years, from 1858 to 1862, he built up a literary reputation such as has not been equalled in Bengal in this century, or in any preceeding century.

In 1862, Madhu Sudan Datta left India for Europe. He remained in Europe five years, was called to the Bar, and composed a book of Bengali sonnets which is well known to our countrymen. In 1867 he returned from Europe and began practice as a barrister in Calcutta.[1] He began well, but the poet was not fitted for the ceaseless endeavours and the prosaic duties of a lawyer's vocation. Madhu Sudan's liabilities increased, and his income dwindled away from year to year. His health failed, and his wife who was true to him to the last began also to suffer in health. Friends ceased to lend when there was no hope of repayment, his two children and his wife suffered the pangs of want before his eyes, and mental

[1] It was in this year that I had the pleasure of first seeing the great poet. A friend who accompanied me was a great admirer of Madhu Sudan's poetry as I myself, and Madhu Sudan did us the favour of reading some portions of his *Meghanad* to us. He was then, what he always was in life, genial, kind-hearted, and good, but careless and improvident. Misfortunes darkly closed over the last years of his life, and within six years after I had seen him so genial and so full of life, Madhu Sudan was no more.

anxiety and bodily infirmities prostrated him in 1873. He laboured in his death-bed to obtain some pecuniary relief, and composed the *Mayakanan,* tinged with the tragic sadness which marked the close of his life.

Jay Krishna Mukherji of Uttarpara gave Madhu Sudan a home in that place, but the poet never recovered from the infirmities that were preying on him. He returned to Calcutta, and without a home to call his own, he took shelter in the charitable hospital of Alipur. Three days before the poet's death, his faithful and much-suffering wife Henrietta breathed her last. Madhu Sudan heard of this and with tears in his eyes repeated the sad lines from Macbeth:

> Tomorrow, and tomorrow, and tomorrow
> Creeps in this petty pace from day to day
> To the last syllable of recorded time. &c.

He died on the 29th June, 1873.

It is not possible within our limits to review the different works of the great poet in detail, and it would be useless to review them cursorily. We will therefore confine our remarks to one of his works, *Meghanad Badh,* which is the greatest literary producttion of this century.

Meghanad Badh Kavya is a story from the *Ramayana,* and relates to the death of Meghanad or Indrajit, the most renowned and powerful of the sons of Ravana. Ravana stole the wife of Rama in his absence, and Rama with his brother Lakshmana crossed with a large army to Ceylon. and invaded Lanka, the capital of Ravana. That great king sent army after army against the besiegers, but the adamantine chain was not broken, and every army and every general sent against the besieging force perished.

The first book opens with a description of Ravana's court, Ravana being sunk in sorrow at the news of the death of his son Birbahu and the destruction of the force sent with him against Rama. Ravana laments the death of all the great warriors who have fallen fighting against the foe, and compares his great city to a festive house in which the lights are one by one extinguished, and the merry sound of harp and flute hushed into silence. At his request the wounded soldier, who had returned from the battle, recounts the deeds of his son in a spirited description which rouses Ravana from his grief. He mounts on the walls of Lanka, reproaches the great ocean for wearing a fetter of stone to cross over Rama's army, and bursts into grief at the sight of Birbahu's corpse stretched on the field of battle. He returns to his palace which is suddenly filled with the voice of woe; Chitrangada the bereaved mother of Birbahu enters. She had been blessed, she says, with one priceless treasure, and had deposited it with the king, even as a dove deposits her young in the dark hollow of trees. The king is the protector of poor men's property, where is poor Chitrangada's treasure now? Ravana is stung with the reproach of his queen and determines on instant war. At his command the city resounds with the sound of war, and horses and elephants and cars and ranks of warriors fill the streets. Indrajit or Meghanad, the sole surviving son of Ravana, hears that his father has resolved to go to war in person. He hastens to Lanka from his country seat, and is permitted by his father to lead the army.[2]

The second book is a description of the heavens. Indra is informed of Meghanad's resolution to fight Rama the next day. Meghanad is invincible in war, and Indra therefore repairs with his wife to the great and benign Uma to pray for the safety of Rama. The conversation that ensues breathes softness, and is worthy of the celestial speakers. Indra pleads the cause of the virtuous Rama, robbed of his wife Sita by the unrighteous Ravana. The wife of Indra takes up the tale, and expatiates on the woes of Sita, now confined in a forest in Lanka, where she weeps day and night for her virtuous lord. Uma answers them with a gracious smile that her lord Siva favours the family of Ravana, and she is powerless to aid Rama. Suddenly a sweet fragrance fills the heavens. and the sound of distant bells is wafted in the air. Rama in distant

[2] *uttar karilā tave cārunetrā devī*
citrāṅgadā ; — "deśavairī nāśe ye samare,
śubhakṣaṇe janma tār ; dhanya vale māni
hena vīr prasūner prasū bhāgyavatī|
* * * *
tava haimasiṁhāsan āśe yujhiche ki dāśarathī ?
* * * *
ke, kaha, e kāl agni jvāliyāche āji laṅkāpure ?
hāy, nāth, nijakarmaphale,
majāle rākṣaskule majilā āpani"|

Lanka is offering his prayers to the benign great Uma. Uma can resist no longer. She repairs to her husband Siva, interrupts him in the midst of his devotions, and obtains a promise that Lakshmana would kill Meghanad on the following day. A message is sent to the goddess Maya who sends down celestial arms to Rama. Rama is full of gratitude to the gods, and enquires how this debt can ever be repaid. Gratitude to gods, truly replies the celestial messenger, consists in supporting and cherishing the poor, in restraining the passions, in living in the paths of virtue, and in adherence to truth. The gift of sandal and flower and silken cloth is despised by gods if the giver is impure.

The third book is one of the most striking and beautiful in the whole work. Pramila, the wife of Meghanad, is disconsolate at the absence of her lord, and longs to leave her country-seat and repair to Lanka where her lord has gone. But the way lies through Rama's army, how can Pramila go? enquires her hand-maid. Pramila, no less favoured with valour than with the beauty, answers with pride and indignation when the mountain-stream leaves her home for the ocean, who can obstruct her course?[3] At her command her maids and attendants, all valiant warriors, conceal or heighten their charms by donning armour and grasping the martial spear, and martial music proclaims the march of the beautious Amazons. Rama will not fight with women, he willingly and even respectfully lends a passage, and the radiant file of valour and beauty passes by, illumining the darkness of the night. Rama, struck with the sight, can scarcely believe that it was not a gorgeous dream.

In fine contrast to the spirited desciptions of the third book, the fourth is full of pathos and tenderness and dwells on the woes of poor Sita, now a captive of

[3] *ruṣilā danav-bālā pramilā rūpasī !*
"ki kahili, vāsanti ? parvat-gṛha chāḍi
bāhirāy yave nadī sindhur uddeśe,
kār hena sādhya ye se rodhe tār gati?
dānav-nandinī āmi, rakṣaḥ-kula-vadhu,
rāvaṇ śvaśur mama, meghnād svāmī, —
āmi ki ḍarāi sakhī, bhikhāri rāghave ?
paśiva laṅkāy āji nija bhuja-bale ;
dekhiva kemane more nivāre nṛmaṇi ?"

Ravana. One lady alone of Ravana's family, Sarama, the wife of Bibhisan, sympathises with her, and repairs to her, and listens to her tales of former days. Sita narrates how after leaving Ayodhya with Rama and Lakshmana, she dwelt in the forest of Panchabati and enjoyed the forest life, how wild flowers bloomed round her cottage and the sweet and joyous chirp of forest birds waked her every morning, how peacocks danced before her and wild deer came in herds as her guests, and how she hospitably entertained these innocent dwellers of the forest. She adorned herself by the margin of the lake with fresh flowers, and her dear lord, pleased with her new dress, would address her as the fairy of the woods ! Will poor Sita meet her lord again and serve him with her affection?[4] The narrator can proceed no further, she weeps bitter tears in woe. Sarama entreats her not to proceed further if those recollections give her pain, but poor Sita would fain proceed. The river filled by the rains pours forth its water on both sides, and the heart that is full of grief finds relief in imparting its grief to others. Sarama cannot choose but listen. In the forest of Panchabati, Sita heard the voice of fairies in sylvan sounds, and saw their dance in the glimmer of the sunbeams on the lake. Sometimes she would walk with Rama by the river, and view on her spacious bosom new heavens, new stars, new radiant moons. Sometimes she would climb a neighbouring hill, and there sit at the feet of Rama, even as a creeper winds round a tree. There she heard from

[4] *yathā gomukhīr mukh haite susvane*
jhare pūta vāridhārā, kahilā jānakī,
madhura-bhāṣiṇī satī ādare sambhāṣi
saramāre, — "hitaiṣiṇī sitār paramā
tumi, sakhī ! pūrvakathā sunivāre yadi
icchā tava, kahi āmi, śuna man diyā|
"chinu morā, sulocane, godāvarī-tīre
kapot kapotī yathā ucca vṛkṣa-cūḍe
bāndhi nīd thāke sukhe ; chinu ghor vane,
nām pañcavaṭī, martye sura-vana-sama|

* * * *

hāy, sakhī, ār ki lo pāva prāṇanāthe ?
ār ki e poḍā āṅkhi e chār janame
dekhive se pā dukhāni-āśār sarase
rājīv ; nayan-maṇi|? he dāruṇ vidhi,
ki pāpe pāpi e dāsī tomār samīpe ?

him various discourses on sacred subjects, even as Uma hears the Vedas and the Puranas from the immortal lips of Siva on mount Kailasa. Will poor Sita hear the music of that voice again ? Even now, in the solitude where she lives, she thinks she hears that voice,—will she never hear that music again? Thus Sita's story goes on. She narrates how in that forest Ravana went in the disguise of a begger and stole her, how Jatayu obstructed his passage, how Sita fell into a swoon and dreamt a dream, how Ravana was victorious and brought Sita to Lanka.

In the fifth book, Maya, the goddess of illusion, sends a dream to Lakshmana. The vision comes to him in the guise of his mother, and asks him to worship Chandi at her temple situated in the north of Lanka. Lakshmana obeys, and Uma appears in person and blesses him. Meghanad also rises with the dawn from the embraces of Pramila, takes an affecting leave of his mother, and repairs to a temple to finish his devotions before going to war.

The sixth book describes the death of Meghanad, and is in our opinion about the weakest in the whole work. Rama has not the heart to let his brother go and do battle with the terrible foe in the heart of Lanka, but at last consents. Lakshmana, dressed in celestial armour, and accompanied by Bibhisan, repairs to Lanka concealed by Maya from the eyes of all. Meghanad suddenly sees his foe in the house of worship, and mistakes him for a god in disguise, but Lakshmana soon undeceives him. He will not even allow Meghanad to don his armour or furnish himself with arms, but Meghanad strikes Lakshmana on the forehead with a cup, and Lakshmana falls into a swoon. Maya revives him, Meghanad is bewildered with strange sights by Maya, and Lakshmana kills him.[5]

[5] *tyaji dhanuḥ, niṣkoṣilā asi mahātejāḥ*
rāmānuj ; jhalasilā phalak-āloke
nayan ! hāyre andha arindam bali
indrajit khaḍgāghāte paḍilā bhūtale
śonitārdra|

* * * *

pramilār vāmetar nayan nācila|
ātma-vismṛtite hāy akasmāt sati
murchilā sindūr-vindu sundar lalāṭe !

It is this portion of the work which we regret the most. The death of Meghanad is not worthy of him. In his anxity to magnify the prowess of his hero the poet forgets that Lakshmana himself is also a warrior. In the original *Ramayana* Lakshmana kills Meghanad in fair fight. Our poet arms Lakshmana with celestial arms, conducts him with another warrior Bibhisan to meet Meghanad who is perfectly unprepared, and even then, Lakshmana is struck down. The poet forgets that the prowess of a warrior is set off best by representing his foeman as worthy of his steel, not by representing him as a child. Homer, from whom our poet frequently borrows his ideas, has not represented Hector as a child in order to adequately describe the prowess of Achilles.

The seventh book is in many respects the sublimest in the work. Siva, who is always inclined in favour of Ravana, is affected at the death of Meghanad, and sends a messenger to fill Ravana with his own prowess to give him a day for revenge. The minor gods descend in a body to assist Rama, nor is he unworthy of celestial assistance. Indra gazes on Rama as on a rival king of the heavens, and Kartikeya sees his own image in the young and bold Lakshmana! Ravana's few dignified yet affecting words to the breaved mother of Meghanad, his address to his army, the spirited conduct and reply of his troops, and the stirring description of the battle that ensues find no parallel in the literature of Bengal. Nowhere, except in the pages of Homer, has battle between more than mortal combatants been so vividly, so powerfully described. Ravana is intent on killing Lakshmana, the slayer of his son, and vain are the attempts to resist his course. Indra, the king of the heavens, cannot hurl his thunder, for a higher power checks him; and Kartikeya retires wonded and smiling when it is whispered to him that Siva has filled Ravana with his own prowess. Rama comes forward, but Ravana wants his brother Lakshnana and will not fight with the elder brother. Hanuman, Sugriva, and the other leaders of Rama's forces quail before Ravana, till the latter at last finds out Lakshmana fighting like a young lion, and they both

mūrchilā rākṣasendrāṇī mandodarī devī
ācambite'! mātṛkole nidrāy kā̃dila
śiśukul ārtanāde|

eagerly mingle in a dubious combat. Gods and men gaze with wonder on the furious battle, and Ravana himself in the midst of the combat pauses in admiration of the valour and prowess of his young and undaunted foe. But none can oppose Ravana to-day, and Lakshmana falls as a falling star, the celestial arms sounding at his fall.[6]

Who shall describe the woes of Rama on the dreadful night after the battle, when Lakshmana lay with other great warriors dead on the field? The eighth book commences with this touching scene. Stars twinkle in the sky, the battle-field is lighted by fires here and there, and Rama bemoans the

[6] *palāila satrāse caudike*
raghusainya, (jal yathā jāṅgāl bhāṅgile
kolāhale);

* * * *

sammukhe rakṣaḥ herilā lakṣmaṇe
devākṛti !

* * * *

"etakṣaṇe re lakṣmaṇ" kahila saroṣe
rāvaṇ "e raṇakṣetre pāinu ki tore
narādham ?"

* * * *

kukṣaṇe sāgar pār haili durmati,
paśili rākṣasālaye corveś dhari,
harili rākṣasa-ratna amūlya jagate"|

* * * *

uttarilā bhīmnādī saumitri-keśarī,
"kṣatrakule janma mama, rakṣakulapati,
nāhi ḍari yame āmi ;"

* * * *

āśu nivāriva śok tava, preri tomā putravar yathā"|
vājila tumul raṇ, cāhilā vismaye
dev nar dohā pāne ;

* * * *

savismaye rakṣarāj kahilā, "vākhāni
virpaṇa tor āmi saumitri-keśarī !"

* * * *

kintu nāhi rakṣā āji mor hāte|"
smari putravare śūr hānilā saroṣe
mahāśakti !

* * * *

bhīmāghāte paḍila bhūtale
lakṣmaṇ nakṣatra yathā ; vājila jhanjhani
deva astra, raktasrote ābhāhīn eve||

death of Lakshmana, the companion of all his toils, the affectionate brother who had left his home, his wife, and his kingdom to attend on him. Uma is affected, and with the permission of her lord Siva, she sends Maya to take Rama to the realm of shades, where Rama's father will tell him the means of reviving Lakshmana to life. The poet borrows from Homer as well from Hindu mythology in his description of hell. Maya takes Rama through regions where sinners are punished after death. He then passes over to those happy regions where the good and virtuous live after death. There he meets his father who tells him of a medicine by which Lakshmana is eventually brought back to life.

The last book describes the funeral of Meghanad. A truce of seven days is granted by Rama at Ravana's request. Pramila mounts the pyre with the corpse of her lord after taking an affecting farewell of her maids and companions, and Ravana bursts into an exclamation of bitter, heart-felt grief, at the loss of the bravest of his warriors and the dearest of his sons.[7]

OTHER POETS

Ranga Lal Banerji was a contemporary of Madhu Sudan, and his first work, *Padminir Upakhyan* came out in the same year with Madhu Sudan's first work, *Sarmishtha,* in 1858. It is a spirited poem on a well-known episode of Rajput history, and was much admired. It was followed by his *Karmadevi* and *Surasundari;* but the fame of the poet was soon eclipsed by

[7]*agrasari rakṣarāj kahilā kātare ;*
"chila āśā meghnād, mudiva antime
e nayandvay āmi tomār sammukhe ;—
* * * *
karvari-gaurav-ravi cira rāhugrāse !
sevinu śivere āmi bahu yatna kari,
labhite ki ei phal ? kemane phiriva
hāyre, ke kave more, phiriva kemane
śūnya laṅkādhāme ār ?
* * * *
hā putra ! hā viraśreṣṭha ! cirajayī raṇe
hā mātaḥ rākṣasa-lakṣmī ! ki pāpe likhilā
e piḍā dāruṇ vidhi rāvaṇer bhāle ?"

the brighter star of Madhu Sudan's genius. Ranga Lal died in 1887.

Among the many poets who are still spared to us, and who continue to enrich the Bengali langauge, we must single out three who stand pre-eminent. Hem Chandra Banerji is the Nestor among the living poets, and was born in 1838. His spirited verse, full of fire and of feeling, won the admiration of the reading public even when the fame of Madhu Sudan was in the ascendant; his patriotic Lyric on India is known by heart to a large circle of readers, and his more ambitious epic, *Britra Sanhar,* is instinct with beauty. But perhaps Nabin Chandra Sen has struck a still deeper chord in the hearts of his countrymen. His first great work. *Palasir Juddha* came like a surprise and a joy to his countrymen, and pleased the reading public by its freshness and vigour and voluptuous sweetness. His great epic on Krishna is still in progress; and his last work *Amitabha* on the life and teachings of Buddha, somewhat after the style of Arnold's *Light of Asia,* sustains and enhances the reputation of the great poet of the Hindu revival of the present day. And lastly, Rabindranath Tagore, youngest son of the venerable Debendra Nath Togore, has distinguisthed himself in poetry, drama and fiction, and his matchless songs are sung in every cultured home in Bengal. Some other poets have also distinguished themselves by their talent and genius. Pandit Siva Nath Sastri's *Nirbasiter Bilap* is a work of great merit, feeling and pathos. Ananda Chandra Mitra is an eccentric genius, and his *Helena Kabya* and *Mitra Kabya* are written with feeling in forcible verse. Krishna Chandra Mazumdar's *Sadbhab Satak* is a wellknown and meritorious work. And Behari Lal Chakrabarti's *Banga Sundari* and other poems display power and feeling. A host of other writers have written meritorious works too much numerous to mention.

It is a sign of the times that female writers have within the last ten or fifteen years entered within the arena of Bengali poetry. Foremost among them should be mentioned the name of Srimati Kamini Sen, now Mrs. K. N. Rai. Her beautiful verses collected under the name of *Alo-o-Chaya,* (Light and Shade), portray the dignity of suffering and of work with delicacy to touch and depth of feeling which are remarkable.

Srimati Man Kumari's *Kusumanjali* is a work of merit. Srimati Girindra Mohini Datta followed with her *Asrukana,* in which the unutterable woes of a Hindu widow are portrayed by one who has felt them, and can express them with power and with eloquence. To the same class belongs the poetry of Rani Mrinalini of Paikpara, whose *Nirjharini* is a marvel from the pen of a young widow of sixteen. Lines like those quoted below[8] strike a chord in every feeling heart, and display a depth of despair and an eloquent simplicity of real sorrow, which our greatest poets can scarcely excel.

Thus the first emotion which has inspired our poetesses, and to which they have given eloquent expression, is one of suffering, of sorrow for the dead, of duty towards the living. These are sacred feelings which most forcibly appeal to the female mind, and naturally enough our poetesses have received their first inspiration from these feelings. We welcome them in the field of literature and poetry, and we hope that as years roll by, and as they take an increasing share of literary work on themselves, they will also take a larger and more comprehensive view of life with all its varied feelings and hopes, joys and sorrows. For real life in its widest manifestation and its deepest meaning is the truest poetry,—real life, painted in those colours which gleam from the heaven of the poet's imagination, and turn the veriest dew drops into pearls !

[8] *dustar e bhavanadi*
kāhār dhariva hāt,
e durgam vanapathe
ke yāve āmār sāth|
* * * *
yadio ekelā āmi
tomarā ta par nao ;
pitār santān yadi,
āmār ta bhāi hao|
ceye dekha sneha vinā
ekṭi bhaginī mare,
dhara abhāgir hāt
tomorā karuṇā kare|
sāthe lao tomāder
e vistīrṇa karma pathe,
bhese yena nāi yāi
śudhu i saṁsar-srote|

CHAPTER XIX

Bankim Chandra Chatterjea and his Novels
(*1838-1894*)

Bankim Chandra is in prose what Madhu Sudan is in verse,—the founder of a new style, the exponent of a new idea. In creative inagination, in gorgeous description, in power to conceive and in skill to describe, Madhu Sudan and Bankim Chandra stand apart from the other writers of the century; they are the first, the second is nowhere. And if the poet's conceptions are more lofty and more sublime, the novelist's creations are more varied, have more of human interest and appeal more touchingly to our softer emotions. The palm must be given to the poet who has bodied forth beings of heaven and earth and the lower rigions in gorgeous verse which sprang into existence like an echo to his ideas; but the reader, after he has traversed the universe on the wings of the mighty poet, will descend with a sense of pleasure to the homely scenes of the novelist, peopled with figures and faces so true and life-like, so sparkling and animated, so rich in their variety and beauty, that they seem to be a world by themselves, created by the will of the great enchanter!

Bankim Chandra was born in 1838, in the same year with the poet Hem Chadra Banerjea. He was the son of Jadab Chandra Chatterjea, who served Government for many years as Deputy Collector, and them retired on pension. Bankim Chandra was educated in the Hooghly College and then in the Presidency College of Calcutta. The Calcutta University was now founded, and Bankim Chandra obtained his degree. and was the first B. A. in India.

In his early years, he with Dina Bandhu Mitra served apprenticeship in the *Prabhakar* journal under the veteran Isvar Chandra Gupta, and Bankim Chandra no doubt acquired much of his ease and facility of writing from this early exercise. Shortly after he had passed his B. A. Examination, he was appointed a Deputy Collector, and he served in different districts. But literary ambition was his ruling passion, and he laboured to achieve something new and great in prose as Madhu Sudan had done in verse. Both were inspired by European models but were sustained by their own genius, and both of them thoroughly assimilated new ideas with the spirit of their country's thought and literature. Madhu Sudan wrote a throughly Hindu epic, though inspired by Homer, and Bankim Chandra wrote novels of Hindu life, though his imagination was fired by the wonderful creations of the prince of modern novelists, Sir Walter Scott.

In 1864, appeared his first historical novel *Durges-Nandini,* and the literary world in Bengal was taken by surprise as it had been three years before, on the publication of *Meghanad.* The boldness of the conception, the skill and grace of the execution, and the variety and richness and surpassing freshness of the figures which live and move and act in this wonderful work, indicated a creative genius of the highest order. Nothing so bold and original had been attempted in Bengali prose, nothing so powerful and so life-like had been executed in Bengali fiction. The venerable Vidyasagar had published his greatest work, *Sitar Banabas,* only two years before, and the work was an adaptation of a Sanscrit drama into Bengali prose. Within two years a new epoch seemed to have dawned on the horizon of Bengali prose literature,—an epoch of original works of the imagination. the like of which Bengal had not known before.

Bankim Chandra did not escape the ridicule which greets every new endeavour. Critics and disappointed writers poured forth their rage on the devoted head of the young author, his style, his conceptions, his story, were all condemned, and he was put down as a denationalized writer, an imitator of European models. But censure and invectives pass off, and a work of real genius stands unmoved like a rock rising above the waves. And after thirty years, the reading public of Bengal acknowledge *Durges-Nandini* to be one of the greatest works in Bengali literature.

The ninteenth century has indeed been a bright century for Bengali literature. But if we were called upon to point out the brightest decade within this century, we should unhesitatingly point to the ten years from 1854 to 1864. More original work, more substantial and lasting work. was done within that decade than either before or after. The eminent

Vidyasagar inaugurated the great widow-marriage movement, and also published his greatest work, *Sitar Banabas,* within this decade. Ram Narayan Tarkaratna began and Dina Bandhu Mitra completed the inauguration of the modern Bengali drama within these years. Madhu Sudan erected his monumental epic in blank verse, and Bankim Chandra founded his new school of fiction, within this memorable decade. It seems as if the literary activity of the century reached its culminating point in the decade closing in 1864. All the best works of the best writers, Vidyasagar, Dina Bandhu, Madhu Sudan and Bankim Chandra were crowded within those ten years.

Having won spurs by his first endeavour, Bankim Chandra did not let the grass under his feet. The weird and wild story of *Kapala Kundala* is perhaps a more wonderful creation of the writer's fancy than even his first great work. And *Mrinalini* which followed, although less sustained than its predecessors, is enlivened by some characters which only a true poet can conceive.

Eight years had now elapsed since the publication of *Durges-Nandini,* and in 1872, Bankim Chandra formed the idea of issuing a first class literary magazine in Bengali. The *Banga Darsan* was accordingly started, and under the editorship of Bankim Chandra, this new magazine rapidly rose in popularity and in fame.

The literary activity of Bankim knew no bounds. Turning aside from his favourite historical romances, Bankim Chandra began to publish in the *Banga Darsan* a social tale which soon attracted thousands of readers. *Bisha Briksha* is the first and most powerful of Bankim Chandra's social novels. Besides this story, continued in the magazine from month to month, other articles animated by wit or replete with information of the most varied kind, and all written in Bankim Chandra's matchless style, soon made the *Banga Darsan* the most popular as it was the most ably written journal of the day. Bankim Chandra now became the sole king of the literary world as Isvar Chandra Gupta had been in an early part of the century, and his long rule continued for over twenty years till the day of his death. During this period Bankim Chandra had no equal and no rival. Madhu Sudan and Dina

Bandhu died in 1873. Akshay Kumar and Vidyasagar had practically retired from literary work. Hem Chandra's greatest and best works had already appeared, and the sound of his harp was now rarely heard. And the younger generation of writers and poets looked up with veneration to the great author of *Durges Nandini* and *Bisha Briksha,* and submitted to his literary sway. Many of them wrote in the *Banga Darsan,* many profited by his example, advice and help, all owned him as their king.[1]

Novels, social and historical, now came out in rapid succession from the fertile pen of the great writer, and his style, always rich and harmonious, became more and more simple

[1] It was in 1872, when the *Banga Darsan* was started, that Bankim Chandra suggested to me to write in Bengali tongue. As the incident throws some light on Bankim Chandra's zeal for his country's literature, the reader will pardon my narrating it. Bankim Chandra was a young Deputy Collector when my father, twenty years his senior, was an honoured and experienced Deputy Collector and was meditating retirement from service. Bankim Chandra was often in the same district with my father, regarded him with the highest respect, and lamented his death, when my father died in the performance of public duty in 1861, like that of an elder and honoured relation. Bankim Chandra always took an interest in me, ten years his junior, and tried to enlist me in the cause of vernacular literature. It was in 1872, when we were talking about the *Banga Darsan,* that I happened to express my appreciation of some of the characters of Bankim's novels. "If you appreciate Bengali literature thus," said the veteran novelist, "why do you not work for it?" "I, write in Bengali !" said I with some surprise, "why, I have never written anything in Bengali. I do not know the Bengali style." "Style !" said he, "why, what a man of your education will write will be Bengali style, and your cultured feelings will do the rest." "You will never live by your writings in English," said he on this or on another occasion, "look at others. Your uncles Gobind Chandra and Shashi Chandra and Madhu Sudan Datta were the best educated men of the Hindu College in their day. Govind Chandra and Shashi Chandra's English poems will never live, Madhu Sudan's Bengali poetry will live as long as the Bengali language will live." These words created a deep impression in me, and two years after this conversation, my first Bengali work, *Banga Bijeta,* was out in 1874. When that work was issuing in another Bengali magazine, Bankim Chandra's *Chandra Sekhar* was appearing in the *Banga Darsan.* He wrote to me of my rival work with his utmost good feeling, and once wrote humorously, "I am crowding my canvas with characters ;—it won't do for a veteran like me to be beaten by a youngster !"

and perfect with age. His *Debi Chaudhurani* and *Ananda Matha* and *Krishna Kanter Will* and other novels, his lighter tales sparkling with the richest humour, and his social, historical and critical essays instinct with thought, found thousands of readers all over Bengal. Whatever he touched glowed with the light of his genius. For a generation the reading world feasted on his unceasing productions; Bengali ladies in their zenana bought every new work of Bankim Chandra as it issued from the press, and young men in schools and colleges knew his latest utterances by heart.[2]

In his later years, he began to write on religious subjects. His great work on Krishna, *Sri Sri Krishnatattva* is written on the same lines as the thoughtful English work *Ecce Homo*, and created a profound sensation in Bengal. Krishna, not as a deity but as a man, as the great Yadava chief who tried to avert war by his wise counsels and ever helped the cause of virtue,—this was the theme of his work. And he proved to the perplexity of his orthodox countrymen that the story of the amours of Krishna finds no mention in the earliest works in Sanscrit literature, and is the mischievous fabrication of later poets. He also took up the study of the Vedas, and felt himself instinctively drawn to the Hindu revival of the present generation, not to the noisy revival of ceremonials and forms and hurtful rules, but to the revival of the purer, deeper and more catholic monotheism of the Hindus which alone can unite and strengthen the nation.

[2] The following passage from *Indira* is a fair specimen of Bankim Chandra's later and simpler style of Bengali prose :—

Anek diner par āmi śvaśur-vāḍī yāitechilām| āmi ūniś vatsare paḍiyāchilām, tathāpi e paryanta śvaśurer ghar kari nāi| tāhār kāran, āmār pitā dhanī, śvaśur daridra| vivāher kichudin parei śaśurar āmāke laite lok pāthāiyachilen, kintu pitā pāthāilen nā ; valilen, "vihāike valio, ye, āge āmār jamātā upārjan karite śikhuk—tār par vadhū laiyā yāiven—ekhan āmār meye laiyā giyā khāoyaiven ki ?|

Bankim Chandra's opinion on the question of the remarriage of Hindu widows is thus explained in his essays on *Samaya* or Equality :—

Āmarā valiva, vidhavā vivāha bhāla o nahe manda o nahe ; sakal viḍhavār vivāha ḥaoyā kadāca bhāla nahe, tave vidhavāganer icchāmata vivāhe adhikār thākā bhāla| ye strī sādhvī, purvapatike āntarik bhālavāsiyachila, se kakhani punarvār pariṇay karite icchā kare nā ;.........kintu yadi kona vidhavā .... patir lokāntar pare punaḥ pariṇaye icchāvatī hayen, tave tini avaśya tāhāte adhikarinī|

Bankim Chandra was made a Rai Bahadur, and a Companion to the Indian Empire by the Government, and died in 1894, lamented by his countrymen. Why is it that so few of our literary men live to the age of three score and ten ? Ram Mohan Roy died at 59 ; Isvar Chandra Gupta at 49 ; Dina Bandhu Mitra at 44 ; Madhu Sudan Datta at 49 ; and Bankim Chandra at 56. The father of Bengali prose literature, Akshay Kumar Datta and Isvar Chandra Vidyasagar lived approximately to the full period of human life, probably because they retired from labours early, and passed their old age in repose. Akshay Kumar died at 66 and Vidyasagar at 71.

These were the kings of our literary world in the present century, and the curious reader can mark the periods of their reign as precisely as the reigns of political sovereigns. I. Ram Mohan Roy reigned from 1815 to 1830, Raja Radha Kanta sharing his reign and ruling over the orthodox section. II. Isvar Chandra Gupta then reigned from 1830 to 1855, Akshay Kumar sharing his rule during the last twelve years. III. The venerable Vidyasagar then ascended the throne with his memorable movement for the re-marriage of Hindu widows, and his rule lasted till 1872, Madhu Sudan and Dina Bandhu and Bankim Chandra sharing the rule. IV. And after a brief and regrettable war over the question of the abolition of polygamy, Vidyasagar abdicated the throne; Madhu Sudan and Dina Bandhu also died in 1873; and Bankim became the sole ruler. and reigned over the literary world for twenty-two years.

Other Writers

The stream of Bengali literature has broadened within the last thirty years, since the date of *Durges Nandini,* and it is difficult within our limits to give any account of this progress and development. The plan which we have pursued in the present work is to confine our remarks to the works only of the leading writers, and to briefly enumerate others who were their collaborators or contemporaries. We will follow this plan in the present chapter.

Magazines. Literary magazines, some of great merit, have multiplied since the days of the *Banga Darsan,* but have mostly been short-lived. The *Jnanankur,* the *Arya Darsan,* the

Bandhab, the *Naba Jiban* and the *Prachar* were excellent magazines, but have ceased to exist. The *Bharati*, the *Nabya Bharat*, the *Sahitya*, the *Sadhana* and the *Janmabhumi* are among the best magazines of the present day. The first named journal is conducted by a lady, Srimati Svrna Kumari Ghoshal, daughter of the venerable Maharshi Debendra Nath Tagore.

NOVELS. The same lady is the author of *Dip Nirvan* and a number of other meritorious novels, and it is a sign of the times that ladies have taken to writing works of fiction as well as of poetry. Sanjib Chandra Chatterjee, brother of the gifted Bankim Chandra, has written *Madhabilata, Kanthamala* and other interesting novels, and Chandra Sekhar Mukerji's *Udbhranta Prem* is also a well-known work. One of the best of modern novels is *Svarnalata* by the late Tarak Nath Ganguli, a simple and pathetic tale of social life in which the characters are powerfully delineated. Indra Nath Banerjea's *Kalpataru* is a humorous but realistic novel of Bengal village life. Damodar Vidyananda has written *Mrinmayi* and a number of other stories, Chandi Charan Banerjea has composed *Monorama's Griha* and other moral domestic tales, and Chandi Charan Sen has published *Nanda Kumar* and other historical novels of orthodox proportions. Pandit Siva Nath Sastri, who has distinguished himself by his poetry and his religious works, has also composed *Mejo Bau* and other meritorious works of fiction; and Rabindranath Tagore, one of the foremost poets of the day, has composed short tales which bear the stamp of his genius. Devi Prasanna Roy Chowdhury has written a number of interesting tales; and the veteran dramatist Mano Mohan Basu has written a meritorious tale about Ranjit Sinha, called *Dulin*. To complete the list, mention may be made of *Banga Bijeta* and three other tales of Indian History by the present writer, as well as his social novels, *Sansar* and *Samaj*.

ESSAYS. Bankim Chandra's thoughtful essays in the *Banaga Darsan* on literary, social and scientific subjects were largely read by his countrymen all over Bengal, and the example he set has been equally followed. Foremost among the essayists of the present day is Kali Prasanna Ghosh of Dacca, whose *Prabhat Chinta* and *Nibhrita Chinta* and other thoughtful essays are widely read and appreciated. Raj

Krishna Mukerjea and Chandra Nath Basu were among the most eminent of Bankim Chandra's collaborators, and have written much that is valuable and thoughtful. Raj Krishna was a man of accurate scholarship and learning, and his *Prabandhas* are marked by a spirit of honest research. Chandra Nath Basu has distinguished himself more by his critical and social essays, like his *Sukuntala Tatva* and his *Hindutva*. Dvijendra Nath Tagore, son of the venerable Debendra Nath Tagore, has written much that is philosophical and thoughtful in his *Tatva Prakas* and other essays. Other writers of lesser note are adding to the stock of our current prose literature.

RELIGION AND ANTIQUITIES. The Asiatic Society continues to publish meritorious editions of ancient Sanscrit works, and many private Pandits and Editors are engaged in the same patriotic task. Our concern however is with Bengali translations and compilations, as they enrich the literature of Bengal, at the same time that they add to the store of our antiquarian knowledge. Pandit Satyavrata Samasrami is the profoundest Vedic scholar in Bengal, and has done much for the spread of knowledge by his editions and translations of *Yajurveda* and *Sama Veda* and his researches in his journals. Mention may also be here made of the edition and translation of the *Rig Veda* by the present writer which caused a sensation among his orthodox countrymen in 1885. An abridged compilation and translation of the entire body of Hindu sacred literature by the same writer is now in course of publication under the title of *Hindu Sastra*.[3] The late Dr. Ram Das Sen published a number of valuable essays on Indian antiquities, and Prafulla Chandra Banerjea has written on the Hindus and the Greeks. Mahesh Chandra Pal and Sita Nath Datta have edited and translated the *Upanishads*, and Kailas Chandra Sinha is a laborious worker in the field of antiquities. Excellent editions and translations of the *Bhagavatgita* have been published by several writers, and the Bangabasi press has presented the reading public with a translation of the *Dharma Sastras*, and also published the *Puranas*. The enthusiastic Sisir Kumar Ghosh is engaged in writing a life of

[3] Since published in two volumes.—Ed.

Chaitanya[4] with all the fervour of a true believer, and other editors and translators, whose names are legion, are engaged in editing, translating and elucidating ancient works. Much of this work is perhaps superficial and even narrow in its scope and object, and is not therefore likely to last. But in spite of all that is sectarian and hollow, the increased attention now bestowed on ancient Hindu scriptures is likely to be attended with the best results, and will have the ultimate effect of drawing the people closer to the nourishing and life-giving faith of the *Upanishads* and the *Vedanta* and the *Bhagavatgita*, which has been, and ever will be, the true faith of the Hindus.

HISTORY. History continues to be studied in English, and little progress has been made in this subject in the Bengali language, except in the matter of school books. Rajani Kanta Gupta's History of the Sepoy War is however a valuable and meritorious work, compiled from original sources.

SCIENTIFIC WORKS. Scientific instruction must also continue to be imparted in this country through the medium of the English language for a long time to come. Abinas Chandra Kabiratna's translations and editions of Sanscrit medical works deserve praise.

BIOGRAPHIES. It is a hopeful sign of the times that there has been a remarkable development in our biographical literature within the present generation. Some meritorious lives of the great men of other nations have been compiled, but the best biographical works in Bengali are the lives of Bengali authors. Pandit Ram Gati Nyayaratna's History of Bengali Literature is a praiseworthy compilation of the lives of our best writers. Nagendra Nath Chatterjea's life of Ram Mohan Roy is a meritorious work, but does not do full justice to its great subject. Mahendra Nath Vidyanidhi's life of Akshay Kumar Datta, Jogendra Nath Basu's life of Madhu Sudan Datta, and Chandi Charan Banerjea's life of Vidyasagar have been referred to in the preceding pages, and are exhaustive and excellent works which leave little to be desired.

POETRY AND DRAMA. Mention has been made of the living dramatists and poets at the close of the last two chapters, and it is needless therefore to enumerate them here.

[4] Published in two volumes under the title of *Lord Gauranga* in 1902. —Ed.

CHAPTER XX

General Intellectual Progress
(*Nineteenth century.*[1])

Progress in Literature in the 19th Century

In the last seven chapters we have traced the progress of Bengali literature in the nineteenth century; it is a progress which we can contemplate with pleasure and with legitimate pride. Not a decade has passed but has brought forth new writers and a marked development. In the early tens and twenties, the great Raja Ram Mohan Roy carried on the work of progress, and the conservative section, headed by the learned Raja Radha Kanta Deb, stood up for ancient rites and customs;. and the result was the formation of a healthy and vigorous prose literature. In the thirties, the poet Isvar Chandra Gupta came on the stage, and enriched Bengali poetry with his flowing and witty and interminable verse, displaying a copious power of the language unsuspected before. In the forties, more earnest workers came on the field; Akshay Kumar's dignified instructions, literary, scientific and moral, were listened to by the advanced school of readers in Bengal, and Isvar Chandra Vidyasagar began his manly work in the cause of educational, social and literary reforms. In the fifties, Ram Narayan Tarkaratna founded the school of modern Bengali drama, and the great Madhu Sudan Datta erected his monumental epic in blank verse. In the sixties, Dina Bandhu Mitra developed dramatic literature, and Bankim Chandra began his new school of fiction and his long and brilliant rule in the world of letters which has terminated only with his death. In the seventies and eighties, new writers rose to distinction, and the genius of Hem Chandra, Nabin Chandra and Rabindranath sheds a lustre on the closing years of this eventful century.

1. For a detailed and upto-date account of the Bengali literature and the social condition of Bengal in this period, see S. K. De : *Bengali Literature in the Nineteenth Century*, Calcutta, 1962.

But when we have spoken of the Bengali writers of the century, we have given only a partial and imperfect account of our country's progress. Englishmen are now the rulers of India, the work of administration and of the courts of justice is carried on in English, higher education is imparted in English, and the English is the one language in which the people of the different provinces in India can communicate with each other. Much of the literary work of our countrymen must therefore be done, and has been done, in English. Our most influential journals must be conducted in English, our best legal works must be composed in English, forensic eloquence can develop itself only in English, constitutional agitation and political work must be carried on in English, and even scientific and historical researches, meant for all the races of India and for European readers, must also be in English. It is necessary therefore to take a cursory view of the work done in English in order to grasp fully the progress made in the present century.

Ram Mohan Roy's English Writings

Raja Ram Mohan Roy was the first worker of the century in English as he was in Bengali; and his controversies with Christian missionaries and his essays on social questions display an extent of knowledge, a power of reasoning, and a mastery over the English language, which surprised distinguished English writers of the day. His controversies have now been wellnigh forgotten, but his translations of the ancient Upanishads into English were among the first attempts to explore into Sanscrit literature and Indian antiquities.

Hindu College and Compositions in English Verse

Raja Ram Mohan Roy helped in the founding of the Hindu College in 1817. The first alumni of the College, however, left the path opened out by the eminent reformer, and for a time indulged in the dream of distingushing themselves in English verse. Fired by the example of such men as Derozio and D. L. Richardson, and impelled by their ardent appreciation of Western literature to which they had found a golden key, they employed their talents in contributing to

English literature. Kasi Prasad Ghosh led the van, and his book of poems in English attracted much attention, as the first attempt of Young Bengal in English poetry. The talented Madhu Sudan Datta followed the example, and his *Captive Ladie* published in Madras in 1849 has already been spoken of.

The Dutt family of Rambagan, sons and nephews of Rasamay Dutt of whom we have spoken before, also entered this field, and soon left all competitors behind. The early effusions of Shashi Chandra Dutt and Govind Chandra Dutt received the deserved compliment of a favourable review in England in Blackwood's Magazine. Shashi Chandra lived to compile historical and other works which have been published in ten volumes, and Govind Chandra with some of his brothers and nephews published the *Dutt Family Album* in England. His talented daughter Taru Dutt then wrote a small collection of *Lays and Ballads of India* which Edmund Gosse brought to the favourable notice of the British public.[4] H. C. Dutt has written his *Lotus Leaves* and G. C. Dutt his *Cherry Blossoms*. O. C. Dutt still delights us with his sonnets and translations from the German and the French, and J. C. Dutt has published the *Indian Pilgrim* in Spenserian verse.

But the dream of earning a fame by contributions to English poetry has now passed away, and Young Bengal has succeeded better in more practical subjects of study. Not long after the time of Raja Ram Mohan Roy, Dr. K. M. Banerjea began his researches into Sanscrit learning. He embraced the Christian religion, and his perfect knowledge of Sanscrit and his command of a graceful English style made him an effective and powerful writer in the field of Indian antiquities. His *Dialogues on Hindu Philosophy* is a profound work, shewing a knowledge of the different systems of Hindu philosophy which very few scholars then possessed. But philosophical and scientific researches fail of their mark when they are made with the object of supporting a particular creed or faith, and Dr. Banerjea's work suffers from this reason, and has never

[4] She also wrote later another volume of verses, *Sheafs Gleaned in French Fields*, an English version of some French poems.—Ed.

been as acceptable to scholars as it otherwise might have been. In his later days, Dr. Banerjea wrote another work. *Aryan Witness,* as profound as his first work, but marked by the same partizanship which takes away from its value.

Dr. Rajendralala Mitra succeeded him in antiquarian and scholastic researches, and soon acquired a European reputation by his learning. He started a cheap magazine called *Bibidhartha Sangraha* in 1851, in Bengali, for spreading useful information among his countrymen, but never succeeded well as a Bengali writer. On the other hand his researches into Indian antiquities were appreciated, and the Government of Bengal employed him, first in surveying the ancient temples of Orissa, and then in examining the temple of Buddha Gaya. Two magnificent works, rich in photographic illustrations, and replete with information about the arts, manners and life of the ancient Hindus, were the result. In the meantime the scattered contributions of the scholar in learned journals were collected and published in two volumes, entitled *Indo-Aryans,* which will remain a monument of his learning.[5]

Works of information

Less ambitious than the eminent Doctors were writers like Bhola Nath Chandra and Rev. Lal Bihari De who have embodied much useful information about their country in their excellent works. Bhola Nath's *Travels of a Hindu* continues to be a most interesting book of information about India, and Lal Bihari's *Bengal Peasant Life* describes the life of the Bengal agriculturist in the guise of a pleasing novel.

Journalism

In journalism, Harish Chandra Mukherjea took the lead about the middle of this century, and the abilitiy, honesty and devotion with which he advocated the claims of his countrymen in the columns of the *Hindu Patriot,* which he founded, received deserved praise and recognition. Kristo Das Pal succeeded Harish Chandra worthily, and laboured for his country with

[5] I take this opportunity of acknowledging my great indebtedness to these volumes in writing my work, *Civilization in Ancient India.*

real talent and sound judgment as the editor of the *Hindu Patriot* until the day of his death.[6]

PUBLIC SPEAKERS

Journalism and public-speaking have gone hand in hand, and the people of Bengal have continued to represent their wishes, and express their views and opinions, in the English language with marked ability. Ram Gopal Ghosh was the first great public speaker in Bengal, and he distinguished himself in the middle of this century by his eloquence and patriotism as the great tribune of the people. Surendra Nath Banerjea is a worthy successor of Ram Gopal Ghosh in the art of public speaking, and in the great work of the political advancement of his country. He has laboured steadily in this cause during the last quarter of the century and has earned for his countrymen an increasing measure of self-government and of representative institutions, and his name will be associated by the future historian of Bengal with the political advancement of the people

POLITICAL ASSOCIATIONS

Political associations, strong in their influence and moderate in their representations, have also flourished in Bengal during this half a century. The British Indian Association, an association of zemindars, is the oldest representative public body in the land. The Indian Association has been founded later on a more popular basis. And lastly, the National Congress unites the representatives and the best educated men from all parts of India in the work of political progress, and carries on a constitutional agitation with moderation and ability.

BRAHMO SAMAJ

Less loud, but not less deep, is the stream of religious and social progress which has broadened since the days of Raja Ram Mohan Roy. The task begun by him has been worthily

[6] Sisir Kumar Ghose published *Amrita Bazar Patrika* from village Amrita Bazar, Jessore, in 1868, first as a Bengali Weekly, a few years later as an English Weekly and then as a daily newspaper from Calcutta.—Ed.

continued by the venerable Devendra Nath Tagore, and the service he has done in continuing the work of moral progress cannot be overestimated. Trained under the moral influence of Debendra Nath, Keshab Chandra Sen founded a new section of the Brahmo Samaj in 1868 ; and he and his followers will always be remembered as pioneers of social reform who, as a body, first ignored the caste system in the present century, and allowed inter-caste marriages. It is a fortunate circumstance that his life and teachings have been recorded by his friend and fellow preacher Pratap Chandra Mazumdar in a work which is the best biographical work in English, written by an Indian. A third and more popular section of the Brahmo Samaj was founded some ten years later, and the talented Siva Nath Sastri and his colleagues are worthily carrying on the work of this advanced section of the Samaj.

The progress of the Brahmo Samaj is an auspicious sign, because the Brahmo Samaj really is an advanced section of the Hindu Samaj. One section of the Brahmos still call themselves Hindus, and all sections have adopted Hindu social and religious rites with some modifications, live Hindu lives, and derive instruction from Hindu sacred works. The social progress of the Brahmos leavens the entire Hindu society, the two communities are drawing closer year after year and when the young society will have counted its first hundred years of existence, its members will be reckoned as a section of advanced Hindus, as the founder of the Samaj meant them to be.

Hindu Reform

Among the Hindus, outside the pale of the Brahmo Samaj, there has been a better understanding among the different sections in recent years. There is a desire on the part of all sections, orthodox and heterodox, to draw closer together, and work for national progress and general good. The domination of the priestly caste which impeded the nation's progress is becoming feebler, the endeavour to bolster up priestly privileges is becoming fainter, the hurtful restrictions of caste are becoming weaker, among advanced Hindus in Bengal. There is a desire to sink social disunion, to ignore modern restrictions, and to turn towards the unpolluted religion and morality of the ancient scriptures to which modern Hindus are now turning for guidance. There is hope in all this, as well as sign of progress.

SCIENCE AND INDUSTRIES

In science, Young Bengal has not succeeded as well as he should have done. Excellent physicians have been turned out from the Medical College, and students distinguished for high proficiency in Chemistry and Physics, Mathematics and Astronomy, have come out of our colleges. But they have as yet given no indication of a capacity for original research. The want of costly instruments in this country may be one reason of this failure, the absence of a class of scientific workers is another. Dr. Mahendra Lal Sarkar's Science Association languishes for want of zealous workers, and the Industrial Association lately started has not yet perceptibly fostered industrial pursuits. Feeble attempts are made now and then in starting new industries, or renovating old ones under new methods. The spinning and weaving of cotton and jute, which grow so plentifully in this country, are done for us in England, and Bengal has not taken any appreciable share in cloth manufacture in which Bombay has set an example. Bengal has not yet distinguished herself in any way in science and industries under the influence of English education.[6]

LAW

Law is a more congenial subject of study for the people of Bengal, and it has been remarked by so high an authority as Sir Henry Maine, that in this subject the nation has shewn something like true merit and genius. The ability, of which Prasanna Kumar Tagore and Rama Prasad Roy and other pleaders of their generation gave evidence, attracted attention, and the highest judical posts under Her Majesty's Government in India were soon won by the talented practioners. Rama Prasad Roy, son of Raja Ram Mohan Roy, was appointed a judge of the High Court of Calcutta, but he did not live to take his seat on the Bench. Sambhunath Pandit

[6] This is a picture of the position at the close of the 19th century when this was written. There has since been considerable progress in all these directions.—Ed.

followed, and later on, the talented Dwarka Nath Mitra distinguished himself by his eoquence, learning and zeal at the Bar, and eventually made one of the soundest and best judges of the High Court. Other able men have succeeded him, and Sir Ramesh Chandra Mitra acted as Chief Justice of Bengal for a period. Among the Bengal Mahommedans, Sayad Amir Ali has won a seat on the Bench of the High Court, and has also distinguished himself by his learned works on the *Life of Mahomet* and on *Mahommedan Law*. But Sayad Amir Ali's works are not the only meritorious legal works composed by Bengalis in modern times. The munificent Prasanna Kumar Tagore has founded a chair for lectures on law; and the lectures, annually delivered, mostly by Indians, form a series of meritorious works on Indian Law.

ADMINISTRATION

In the work of general administration, the people of the country have been admitted to take a share with greater caution, their efforts have been more arduous and prolonged, and their success therefore is a matter of greater congratulation. The administration of India is unconsciously affected by party triumphs in England, and it was when a strong and healthy liberal reaction gave the seats in the Parliament to the real representatives of the British nation in 1832, that a real share in administrative work in India was for the first time given to the people of Bengal by Lord William Bentinck. The class of men whom he appointed, Sub-Judges and Deputy Collectors, soon distinguished themselves by their ability, capacity for work, and knowledge of their country, and the creation of these appointments has strengthened the Government, and brought British rule more in touch with the people.

In 1852. Lord Russell revived the question of Reform in England, and the second Reform Bill was passed in 1867. It was within these years that the covenanted Civil Service was thrown open to all Her Majesty's subjects, and the first Indian entered the Civil service. In 1862, Satyendra Nath Tagore, a son of the venerable Devendra Nath Tagore, passed the open Competition held in England for admission into the Civil Service of India. An ungenerous alteration in the system of marking, which immediately followed, prevented other Indians from succeeding for some years. In 1869 however, three other Bengalis and one of Bombay passed the Open Competition. And since their time, young men are proceeding to England in increasing numbers, year after year, to compete for the Civil Service, to qualify themselves for the Bar or as Doctors or Engineering, or merely to complete their general education.

The third and last Reform act, equalizing franchise in counties and boroughs, was passed in England in 1885. The wave of liberal reaction reached, as on previous occasions, as far as India, the local Self-Government Act and the Municipal Act of Lord Ripon were passed between 1884 and 1886, and the people were thus admitted to a larger share in the administration of local affairs.

Appointment to higher services after examinations in England

The training of our young men in England has been attended with beneficial results. Men who have entered the higher ranks of services by passing examinations in England have taken, as Civilians, Doctors or Engineers, a responsible share in tbe work of administration to which their countrymen generally are not admitted. Bengali Civilians have held the posts of District Officers, District Judges and Divisional Commissioners, Bengali Medical men have held the post of Civil Surgeons, and Engineers have risen to the rank of Executive Engineers. This direct enlargement of the share taken by the people of Bengal in the administration of their country benefits the people, and makes British rule stronger and more popular in India.

Bar

No less signal is the service rendered by those who have came out as members of the Bar. Mano Mohan Ghose, who went to England with Satyendra Nath Tagore, came out as the first Bengali Barrister. The poet Madhu Sudan Datta came out about the same time, and Woomesh Chandra Bonnerjea came out shortly after, in 1868. Madhu Sudan is dead; but Ghose and Bonnerjea are among the Nestors of the Bar at the present time. The service they have rendered to the country by helping the cause of justice and thus improving administration is great. But the service which they have rendered as workers for the political advancement of their countrymen is still more valuable. Younger Barristers are walking in their foot-steps, and our country owes and will continue to owe much to her talented and patriotic sons who have taken to the legal profession.

Social Results of visit to Europe

For the rest the great rush of our young men to Europe is silently causing a reform in our social rules. These young men ask no sanction from the leaders of the caste organization when they cross the seas and proceed to Europe, or when they return and live among their friends and relations, and occasionally marry out of caste. Orthodox Hindu society is gradually becoming familiarized with such departures from old and cast-iron rules, and silently accepts the fact that a living society must be progressive. The best way to do a thing is to do it, says the proverb, and Young Bengal, educated in Europe, knows the truth of this proverb. Social reforms for which men like the venerable Vidyasagar spent the best portions of their lives are being effected unostentatiously, without discussion in pamphlets and journals, and without the sanction of learned conclaves of Pandits. A deed done is worth more than years of idle discussion; Hindu society feels it, and is gradually accepting the inevitable.

Conclusion

Young Bengal has his faults, and is not in want of "candid friends" to point them out to him. But his critics, who are so severe on his failings, know little of his difficulties and his struggles. Within the present century, Young Bengal has endeavoured to form a healthy national literature, has striven for social and religious reforms in the light of the ancient Hindu scriptures, has distinguished itself in law and administration, and works hopefully and manfully for the good of the country. There is reason for hope in all this, but there is more reason for earnest work in the future; and it rests entirely with ourselves to work out the results already foreshadowed. There is not a nation in Europe which has not shaped its own destiny by centuries of hard and arduous toil in past ages. We live in happier times, and under the influence of a healthier liberal opinion, and it rests with ourselves whether under these influences, and under the generous guidence of England, we shall move onward in the path of national progress, as all English colonies are doing in this age of progress.

APPENDIX

"The Literature of Bengal"

The following extracts are reproduced from *Life and Work of R. C. Dutt* by J. N. Gupta, London, 1911:—

The little book on *The Literature of Bengal* is perhaps the most notable performance of Mr. Dutt in English during the period of his apprenticeship. In undertaking this work, Mr. Dutt, as in other fields, set up before him a "national" standard. "To trace as far as possible the history of the people, as reflected in the literature of Bengal," was his object. For it was a favourite contention of his that the "literature of every country, slowly expanding through successive ages, reflects accurately the manners and customs, the doings, and the thoughts of the people. And thus, although no works of a purely historical character had been left behind by the people of ancient India, it is possible to gain from their works on literature and religion a fairly accurate idea of their civilisation, and the progress of their intellect and social institutions." The wider and more comprehensive task of reconstructing the history of ancient India, on the basis of her past literature, he took up later in life For the present he confined himself to a humbler sphere.

The first edition of the book came out in 1877, and the author assumed the *nom de guerre* of Ar. Cy. Dac. To his uncle, Rai Shoshee Ch. Dutt Bahadur, to whom, as we have seen, he owed so much of his literary predilections, he gratefully dedicated the work as a token of esteem.. A much improved and enlarged edition, under his own name, appreared later on, in 1896.

The great merit of the work is that it was the first scientific attempt to write a history of our national life and literature. And we have only to compare this book with the previous work on the same subject in the vernacular, by Pandit Ramgati Nayaratna, to appreciate the great advance made in critical method. It is true that the work does not bear the impress of much original research either in the field of the vexed question of the origin of the Bengali language or the disputed authorship of the works of the earliest period of that literature, nor is his canvas large enough to enable him to do justice to even the most important figures of his narrative. But nevertheless the book is marked by a breadth of vision, and a firm grasp of the main stages of the intellectual life of Bengal from the twelfth century to the present day, and of the outstanding factors which have moulded that life.

According to Mr. Dutt, the history of Bengali literature, as of the Bengali people, naturally divides itself into three distinct periods, viz. :—

"First, the period of lyrical poetry, extending from the twelfth to the end of the fifteenth century of the Christian era. The representative men of this period are Jayadeva, Vidyapati, and Chandidasa. A host of other poets of smaller note flourished in this period.

Second, the period of classical influence, extending from the beginning of the sixteenth century to the end of the eighteenth century The representative men of this period are the great Chaitanya, Krittibas, Mukunda Ram, Kasi Ram Das, the great Raghunath, and Bharat Chunder Roy.

Third, the period of European influence, being the period in which we are living, and commencing with the nineteenth century. The central figures of this period are the great Ram Mohan Roy, Akshay Kumar Dutt, Isvar Chandra Vidyasagar, Isvar Chandra Gupta, Michael Madhu Sudan Dutt, Hem Chandra Banerjea, Dina Bandhu Mittra, and Bankim Chandra Chatterjea.

The first period presents us with a mass of love songs about Krishna and Radhika, composed with deep feeling. The second period presents us with more earnest thinking and work, with the rise of a new religion, the cultivation of literature in the classical style, and investigations into Sanskrit philosophy. The last period strikes us with an outburst of multifarious feelings and the display of a free, daring intellect. The second period is an improvement on the first, and the third beats all. For we do not hesitate to say that the *Meghnad Badh Kavya* leaves Chandi and Vidyasundar as far behind, as Chandi and Vidyasundar leave behind the simple though sweet strains of Vidyapati and Chandi Das.

Up to the end of the fifteenth century our literature consisted simply of songs feelingly sung, about the amours of Krishna and Radhika. But the national mind was now awakened. The first effect of this change was the introduction of a new religion, deep and earnest in its character, and far-reaching in its consequences. In literature, too, there was a hankering for something vaster and nobler than what had been inherited from the preceding ages; there was an energy capable of something greater than the composition of songs. At such a crisis, the nation turned its eyes to the hitherto virgin mine of Sanskrit literature, and that was a mine which satisfied the highest aspiration, and rewarded the utmost endeavour. From this time forward then, we find our authors producing not simply songs as hitherto, but big tomes of poetry, all in the classical style. The two great epics in Sanskrit, the "Ramayana" and the "Mahabharata," were translated into Bengali, and original epics like the "Chandi" of Mukunda Ram and the "Annada Mangal" of Bharat were written in the classical style. Nor was the national mind satisfied with poetry alone. The abstrusest questions of law and metaphysics, and deep and subtle problems of psychology, engaged the attention of the great Raghunath and other earnest workers of the school of Nadia. Thus the revolution of the sixteenth century had a threefold effect, viz. religious, literary, and philosophical."

But it is his observations on the latest period that deserve our closest attention.

"The conquest of Bengal by the English [says he in the first edition of his work] was not only a political revolution, but ushered in a greater revolution in thoughts and ideas, in religion and society. We cannot describe the great change better than by stating that English conquest and English education may be supposed to have removed Bengal from the moral atmosphere of Asia to that of Europe. All the great events which have influenced European thought within the last one hundred years have also told, however feeble their effect may be, on the formation of the intellect of modern Bengal. The Independence of America, the French Revolution, the war of Italian independence, the teachings of history, the vigour and freedom of English literature and English thought, the great effort of the French intellect in the eighteenth century, the results of German labour in the field of philology and ancient history—Positivism, Utilitarianism, Darwinism—all these have influenced and shaped the intellect of modern Bengal. In the same degree all the great influences which told on the Bengali mind in previous centuries, the faith of Krishna, the faith of Chandi or Kali, the preachings of Chaitanya, the belief in the truth of Hinduism and the sacredness of the Shastras, the unquestioning obedience to despotic power in all its phases, the faith in the divine right of royalty and in the innate greatness of princes and princesses—all these ancient habits and creeds have exercised feebler and yet feebler influences on the modern Bengali intellect. In habits, in tastes, in feeling, freedom and vigour and patriarchal institutions, our literature therefore has underegone a corresponding change. The classical Sanskrit taste has given place to the European. From the stories of gods and goddesses, kings and queens, princes, and princesses, we have learned to descend to the humble walks of life, to sympathise with a common citizen or even a common peasant. From an admiration of a symmetrical uniformity we have descended to an appreciation of the strength and freedom of individuality. From admiring the grandeur and glory of the great, we now willingly turn to appreciate liberty and resistance in the lowly."

These passages he omitted from his second edition, and rightly, for although they define accurately his own mental outlook and his position in the hierarchy of Indian thinkers and writers, yet they can scarcely be said to present a correct view of the Bengali literature of the nineteenth century.

"Every revolution [he goes on to say] is attended with vigour, and the present one is no exception to the rule. Nowhere in the annals of Bengali literature are so many or so bright names found crowded together in the limited space of one century as those of Ram Mohan Roy, Akshay Kumar Dutt, Isvar Chandra Vidyasagar, Isvar Candra Gupta, Michael Madhu Sudan Dutt, Hem Chandra Banerjea, Bankim Chandra Chatterjee, and Dina Bandhu Mittra. Within the three quarters of the present century, prose, blank verse, historical fiction, and drama have been introduced for the first time in the Bengali literature, and works of imagination have been written which leave the highest and best efforts of previous centuries far behind."

In his second edition, he added a brief but searching summary of the wonderful intellectual revolution which followed the first introductioin of English education into Bengal...

Of his critical estimates, the best is his appreciation of Raja Ram Mohan Roy, and he is generally on firm ground when he deals with kindred spirits like the great Raja or Isvar Chandra, or in a narrower sphere, Akshay Kumar Dutt. But his estimate of Madhu Sudan as the greatest literary genius of Bengal will hardly be shared by most competent critics, for it is doubtful whether Madhu Sudan possessed the supreme gift of inspiration, the inevitableness of true art in the same degree as did Bankim Chandra who is by many acknowledged to be the king of Bengali literature of the nineteenth century. In his best creations like "Chandra Sekhar," or "Krishna Kanta's Will," Bankim Chandra gave us unalloyed gold ; but there is not a page in the "Meghanath Badha" where the purer metal is not alloyed with tinsel of a baser stuff.

The book received a warm welcome, and a scholar like Sir William Hunter quoted freely from it in his standard work on the "Indian Empire." On the appearance of his second edition *The Englishman* published a most appreciative notice.

"He has now returned [said *The Englishman*] to his first love, the love of his motherland, and, with increased knowledge and wider experience, gives us an almost rewritten and greatly improved second edition of his work *The Literature of Bengal*. It will surprise many to learn that Bengali has a literature worth writing about. To most people it consists of one insipid and lubric work, the Vidya Sundar of Bharat Chandra, the writings of Vidyasagar, of Bankim Chatterjee's modern novels, of a few examination text-books, and of the Indian press. We fear that of these the only ones ever read by such persons are the examination text-books, read once and then worthily abandoned for ever. The others are forgotten or ignored, and much is lost thereby. But Bengal has a literature, dating from the fourteenth century, full of interest not only to the student, but also to the general readers. We need not follow Mr. Dutt through the other chapters of his interesting volume. It is sufficient to refer to those of our readers who wish to know the inner life, the thoughts, the feelings, the real life of Bengal—not the bastard imitation of English habits and, too often, English vices, which floats like a scum one the surface of our great cities—to his book. After all, the songs of a people have more power than its laws, and a young civilian can learn better to gain the hearts of his people from an hour's study of *The Literature of Bengal* than from years of application to the history of the fortunes of A and Z in the Penal Code."

Its influence reached even England, and shortly after the publication of this book the following very appreciative article on the "New Literature of Bengal" appeared in the columns of *The Times.*

"One of the striking products of British rule in India is the vernacular literature of the provinces. With the English and French works of Indian authors, some of them of considerable merit, the European world is more or less acquainted. But we scarcely realise the fact that such works are altogether insignificant compared with the vast and vigorous growth of literature in the Indian language. That growth is not confined to one part of India or another; where it has found literary dialects ready for its use, it has developed them; where it has not found literary dialects, it has created them. Varieties of human speech never reduced to writings have been furnished with alphabets and printed types. Rude or poor dialects only used for song have been amplified into prose. Better furnished dialects have been still further enriched from the classical languages of India, and now supply vehicles for the complex problems of philosophy, science, and modern thought. Nowhere has the activity been greater than in Lower Bengal.

To those who would study this subject as a whole, and who desire to understand the intense activity of the Indian mind under British rule, we could recommend Mr. R. C. Dutt's recently published volume on "The Literature of Bengal." Mr. Dutt springs himself from a distinguished literary family, and he has well maintained its reputation both in prose and verse. The conspicuous merit of his book is its frank acknowledgment that no literary success which an Indian can make in English or any exotic tongue, is to be compared as regards its value to his countrymen with first-class work in his own language. It is this instinct of literary patriotism which animates the best Bengali writers, and which has within a century created a prose literary language for Bengal."

INDEX

[1]The names of authors and works have been indexed. Figures indicate pages. Footnotes are indicated with asterisks.